CHINA: THE CONSUMER REVOLUTION

CHINA: THE CONSUMER REVOLUTION

By

Conghua Li

Deloitte & Touche Consulting Group

John Wiley & Sons (Asia) Pte Ltd
Singapore • New York • Chichester • Brisbane • Toronto • Weinheim

Copyright © 1998 by Deloitte & Touche Consulting Group.
Published by John Wiley & Sons (Asia) Pte Ltd.
2 Clementi Loop #02-01 Jin Xing Distripark, Singapore 129809, Singapore.

Other Wiley Editorial Offices

John Wiley & Sons, Inc.
605 Third Avenue, New York, NY 10158-0012, USA

Jacaranda Wiley Ltd
33 Park Road, (PO Box 1226) Milton, Queensland 4064, Australia

John Wiley & Sons (Canada) Ltd
22 Worcester Road, Rexdale, Ontario M9W ILI, Canada

John Wiley & Sons Ltd
Baffins Lane, Chichester, West Sussex PO 19 IUD, England

Library of Congress Cataloging-in-Publication Data

Li, Conghua
    China : the consumer revolution / by Conghua Li.
        p. cm.
    Includes index.
    ISBN 0-471-24862-2
    1. Consumers — China. 2. Consumption (Economics) — China.
I. Title.
HC430.C6L48 1997   97–35917
381.3'0951—dc21   CIP

Printed in the Republic of Singapore
10 9 8 7 6 5 4 3 2

Contents

Foreword   ix
Acknowledgments   xi
Introduction   xv

Chapter 1 **The Consumer Revolution**   1
           The world's fastest growing consumer society   2
           Underlying social and cultural values   8
           The forces shaping future consumption   20

Chapter 2 **Generations Apart**   49
           New wave consumers   50
           The s-generation comes of age   51
           Young and middle aged rural consumers   59
           The 60+ consumer   69

Chapter 3 **Pioneering**   77
           New consumer centers   78
           Satellite cities   80
           New coastal cities   87
           Resource-rich regions   94

Chapter 4 **New Times, New Realities**   99
           Life in transition   100
           Three-dimensional living   100
           A nation on the move   109
           Apartment-bound   114

Chapter 5 **Luxuries Become Essentials**   119
           What they want   120
           Ambience   123
           Efficiency   131
           Health   143
           Status   152

Chapter 6 **As For The Necessities**   159
           Shifting priorities   160
           Home improvement   160
           Investment and insurance   171
           Education and telecommunications   183

Chapter 7 **Taking The Plunge**   191
           Taking the plunge   192
           Approaches in practice   193
           Stages of business development   198
           Keys to success   205
           Challenges ahead   210

Glossary   225

References   229

Index   237

Figure I.1   A framework for analyzing the Chinese consumer

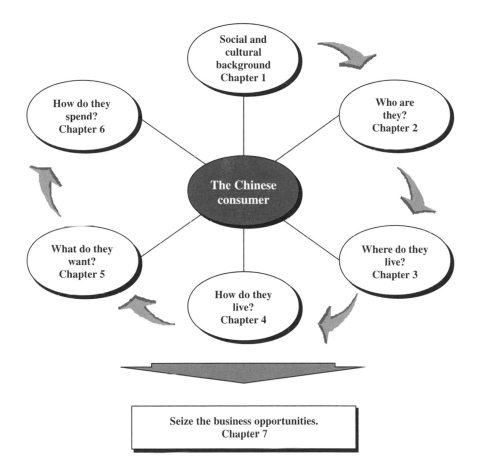

Foreword

Conghua Li, the author of this book, considers himself a student in the field. Indeed he is an experienced management consultant with a deep understanding and has first-hand expertise on the consumers and the consumer intensive industries in China. He combines the professional strengths gained both from the East and from the West, and is committed to assisting both global and local businesses to succeed in the fast changing market.

China's economy is the second largest in the world. It is expected to overtake that of the United States within the next 20 years. Considering their economic contribution to the nation's GDP, the State-owned companies in China have become a minority. The number of international companies established in China has already surpassed 250,000. This economic transformation is now embracing a far reaching social transformation.

The marketplace in China is increasingly consumer driven. Chinese consumers are now taking on responsibilities in the areas of housing, education, insurance and their personal long-term financial well-being. In only five years, the consumer market in the city of Shanghai alone reached a level of development comparable to that which was reached by Taiwan in more than 20 years.

The keys to the success of doing business in China have shifted increasingly from dealing with red tape and relationships to dealing with the changing consumer demand and the fierce global competition in the local marketplace.

Deloitte & Touche Consulting Group is confident about the future business potential in this dynamic marketplace. With over 10,000 management consulting professionals around the world, we are committed to assisting our clients in succeeding in this challenging and exciting business environment.

As the new millennium dawns, a new consumer society is waking in the East. It provides unprecedented opportunities to the world. Its sheer size and unparalleled dynamics will redefine the consumer market as we know it today.

China is a different world. To succeed, it is important for all of us to embrace and learn about this market.

Pat A. Loconto
Chief Executive Officer
Deloitte & Touche Consulting Group
July 1997, New York, NY, USA

Acknowledgments

This work would not have been possible without the sincere and effective support of a large number of people within and outside China.

As I was traveling across China conducting first hand research for this book, hundreds of people spent time with me and provided information. These people told me stories about their personal life, shared their wishes and concerns, invited me into their homes, provided me with valuable publicly available information materials, pointed out relevant public information sources, and further introduced me to relevant people. They revealed their business operations, personal lives, feelings and consumption behaviors. They were from a wide range of social and professional backgrounds — senior executives of international companies, owners of local private companies, governmental officers, academia at universities, researchers at think tanks, journalists, editors, farmers, workers, traders on the markets, school teachers, taxi drivers, seniors, housewives, teenagers, children, night club managers, etc.

While I am grateful to all of these people, I especially want to express my sincere thanks to the following: in Beijing, Ms. Wenjing Bian, Ms. Daofu Chen, Ms. Boyan Gao, Ms. Chuenqing Jiang, Prof. Hong Kuang, Prof. Boxiong Lan, Dr. Gervais Lavoie, Dr. Li Liao, Mr. Weimin Li, Mr. Yansheng Li, Mr. Zengming Li, Mr. Frank Liu, Dr. Jianhua Lu, Mr. Xinyuan Mo, Mr. Yijian Qian, Mr. Frank Wang, Mr. Yilong Wang, Ms. Suning Wang, Mr. Binggong Yan, Ms. Binglian Yan, Ms. Bingsu Yan, Ms. Bingzhuang Yan, Mr. David Zhang, Dr. Taowei Zhang, Dr. Ping Zhao, Mr. Yimin Zhou; in Chengdu, Mr. Zhong Cao, Mr. Chuande Wang, Mr. Jun Wen, Ms. Zhehua Zhang; in Dalian, Mr. Haiying Bao, Mr. Benji Li, Mr. Min Liu, Prof. Chengde Luan, Mr. Junwu Tu, Prof. Haixing Wang,

Prof. Gongqian Zhang, Mr. Weizhong Zhang; in Guangzhou, Mr. Liming Chen, Mr. Zhuechao Chen, Mr. Hongye Ja, Ms. Shuangrong Li, Mr. Xusen Zhang; in Harbin, Ms. Kaiyu Ma, Ms. Junhui Wang; in Kunming, Mr. Gao Liu, Ms. Qinxian Wang, Mr. Kaiping Xu, Mr. Yan Zhao, Mr. Desheng Zhao; in Shanghai, Mr. Iwan Evans, Mr. Junde Fei, Mr. Zhaohui Gong, Mr. Fugui Huang, Mr. Ming Li, Mr. Jianjun Meng, Mr. Rongguo Yang, Mr. Qiosheng Zhao, Mr. Weisheng Zhao; in Shenzhen, Mr. Kelly W.K. Chan, Mr. Zhisheng Chen, Mr. Mingqing Fu, Dr. Wanda Guo, Ms. Lidan Huang, Mr. Huelin Huang, Mr. Di Tian, Mr. Liangcheng Wu; in Urumqi, Ms. Hongyu Qou, Mr. Qingyu Gou, Mr. Dezheng Li, Ms. Jumei Qiao, Ms. Ruxangul, Mr. Wanli Tang, Ms. Xialipa, Ms. Lanzhen Zhang, Ms. Han Zhu; in Wuhan, Ms. Yun Liu; in Xian, Mr. Deting Wu, Mr. Ping Wu, Ms. Wen Xu; in Bremen, Dr. Xinfu Li, Ms. Qianzhi Li; in Hong Kong, Mr. Mumtaz Ahmed, Mr. Anthony Chang, Mr. Tie Mao, Dr. Shaomin Li, Prof. David K. Tse; in Silkeborg, Mr. Lars Holm; and in Toronto, Ms. Mary Kwok, Ms. Qin Luo, Mr. Huanli Lu, Ms. Fong Yuan, Mr. Pingnan Yuan.

During the writing and reviewing period, I received strong support from a large number of individuals. These individuals include internationally renowned experts in the field, my professional writer, colleagues, personal friends and family. I want to first express my special thanks to my professional writer Lawrence Jeffery who helped me to apply engaging language in addressing the strategic concerns of senior business executives. Together we spent night after night fine-tuning this book.

It is my honor to especially thank the reviewers of the manuscript involved at different stages of the development of this book: in Barcelona/Shanghai, Prof. Pedro Nueno; in Beijing, Mr. Clarence Kwan, Mr. Mark Rowswell (also in Toronto); in Boston, Prof. George C. Lodge, Prof. Daniel Quinn Mills, Prof. John A. Quelch; in Dallas, Mr. Richard C. Bartlett; in Hong Kong, Mr. Patrick Cheng, Mr. Frank

Davis, Mr. Ted T. Lee; in London, Mr. Barry Hedley; in Melbourne, Mr. Scott L. Fraser; in New York, Mr. Keith Ferrazzi, Mr. David Read; in Palo Alto, Mr. Lee S. Ting; in Philadephia, Mr. Buzz Plesser; in Phoenix, Mr. Richard Furash; in Shanghai, Mr. Chris Lu, Mr. Authur Tse; in Singapore, Dr. Mark Mobius, Mr. Nick Wallwork; in Tokyo, Dr. Kenichi Ohmae; and in Toronto, Mr. Graham Baragwanath, Mr. Frank Brown, Ms. Sigrid Feser, Prof. Bernard Michael Frolic, Ms. Qin Luo, Mr. Marvin Stemeroff, Mr. Christian Stephan, Mr. Walter Thompson, Mr. Jiangong Xiao, Ms. Loretta Yuen.

This book was produced in a relatively short time frame. I received large amounts of assistance from all directions. However the most crucial contribution has been from the staff at John Wiley & Sons Asia Pte Ltd and Cotter Communications in Singapore. I would like to thank Ms. Jane Cotter, Ms. Janis Soo and Mr. Nick Wallwork for their assistance.

I shall never forget the support from my wife Simone Stephenson Li prior and during the intense working period in producing this book. I would not have come to commence this work without her professional inspiration. I want to thank her for using her natural observational skills, for her input in researching facts, discussing ideas, reviewing the manuscript and for her continued support and enthusiasm.

Last but not least, I want to point out that without the support of the Deloitte & Touche Consulting Group, this book would not have been completed. I have received support from many of my colleagues in the worldwide network of Deloitte Touche Tohmatsu International. While I have previously expressed my gratitude to some of them for their particular contributions, I would like to again express my deep thanks to Mr. Graham Baragwanath for his continued championship, encouragement and professional input. I would also like to thank, in Hong Kong, Ms. Canny Ma, Ms. Lisa McGahan; and in Toronto, Ms. Elizabeth Appleton, Mr. Greg James, Mr. Mike

Nethercott, Ms. Heather Owen and Ms. Helen Zubrinic for their assistance in the entire process.

Introduction

China's economy and business environment is increasingly being driven by the domestic consumer. The developments in China's economy, and the profound implications of those developments on international businesses today, and into the next century, are unparalleled in world history.

The purpose of this book is to explore and explain as clearly and simply as possible, the extraordinary consumer revolution that has grown out of China's current economic boom. Figure I.1 is a schematic outline of the material in this book. At a glance, it shows the approach I have taken to the many complex social, cultural and economic issues present in the China market.

Anyone interested in business or consumer societies will find the story of China's consumer revolution fascinating. For business strategists interested in entering the China market, or already in the China market and wishing to expand, this information will provide an effective overview of many key consumer issues relevant to all types of businesses including consumer goods, pharmaceuticals, telecommunications, financial services, retail, wholesale, residential construction and agri-businesses. There are many other important issues that business strategists need to understand, for example, socio-political issues, legal issues, environmental issues and risk issues. Nevertheless I have focused my attention on the "pure" consumer-related issues in this book.

I am confident that the consumer trends and their business implications examined in this book will remain relevant until at least year 2010. Some may question my confidence, and the conclusions I draw from available facts and statistical references. Of course, no one knows what the future will bring. I do, however, have a deep understanding for the country of my birth and its people. Futhermore, my view of China has also been shaped by many years of professional experiences in the West, and a far ranging analysis of the present scene in China, both statistical and first hand. I am sure that much of this material will be surprising and confounding to readers in the West, but no more surprising or confounding than it has been and continues to be for China's consumers themselves. I am confident of my insights and conclusions, and invite readers to approach this material with an open mind, free of prejudice or expectation.

Conghua Li
July 1997

Provinces of China

1. 北京市 (BEIJING)
2. 天津市 (TIANJIN)
3. 上海市 (SHANGHAI)
4. 重慶市 (CHONGQING)
5. 寧夏回族自治區 (NINGXIA)

黑龍江省
HEILONGJIANG

吉林省
JILIN

遼寧省
LIAONING

內蒙古自治區
INNER MONGOLIA

山東省
SHANDONG

江蘇省
JIANGSU

安徽省
ANHUI

浙江省
ZHEJIANG

福建省
FUJIAN

台灣
TAIWAN

河北省
HEBEI

山西省
SHANXI

河南省
HENAN

湖北省
HUBEI

江西省
JIANGXI

廣東省
GUANGDONG

香港
HONG KONG

陝西省
SHAANXI

湖南省
HUNAN

貴州省
GUIZHOU

廣西壯族自治區
GUANGXI

海南省
HAINAN

甘肅省
GANSU

四川省
SICHUAN

雲南省
YUNNAN

青海省
QINGHAI

新疆維吾爾自治區
XINJIANG

西藏自治區
TIBET

Major Cities of China

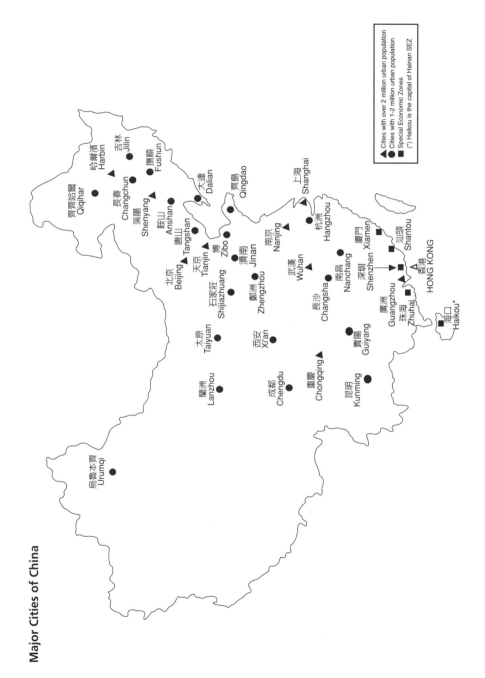

Legend:
▲ Cities with over 2 million urban population
● Cities with 1–2 million urban population
■ Special Economic Zones
(*) Haikou is the capital of Hainan SEZ

齊齊哈爾 Qiqihar
哈爾濱 Harbin
吉林 Jilin
撫順 Fushun
長春 Changchun
瀋陽 Shenyang
大連 Dalian
青島 Qingdao
上海 Shanghai
鞍山 Anshan
唐山 Tangshan
北京 Beijing
天津 Tianjin
博 Zibo
濟南 Jinan
南京 Nanjing
杭州 Hangzhou
廈門 Xiamen
汕頭 Shantou
石家莊 Shijiazhuang
鄭州 Zhengzhou
武漢 Wuhan
南昌 Nanchang
深圳 Shenzhen
香港 HONG KONG
太原 Taiyuan
西安 Xi'an
長沙 Changsha
廣州 Guangzhou
珠海 Zhuhai
海口 Haikou*
蘭州 Lanzhou
成都 Chengdu
重慶 Chongqing
貴陽 Guiyang
昆明 Kunming
烏魯木齊 Urumqi

Advance Praise for
China: The Consumer Revolution

"Conghua Li's new book gives outsiders a fascinating insight into what is happening in China's consumer market today. Foreign companies trying to take advantage of the vast Chinese market are often confronted with the difficulties of reaching the right target buyers. Li's book objectively analyzes the structure and characteristics of the Chinese consumer market, and concludes that the fruits of this attractive market are available only when you understand the delicate nuances of the regional, income class and generational niches. The puzzles of the Chinese consumers – young and yet sophisticated, low income and yet high purchasing power and strong appetite for consumption — are explained in a way nobody else has ever done. This is a must read for those who have their stakes vested in the most dynamic and difficult, and yet the last remaining, consumer utopia of the world."

Kenichi Ohmae

Ohmae and Associates, Chancellor's Professor of Public Policy of UCLA, Author of *The Borderless World* and *The Mind of the Strategist*

"This book is one of the most incisive studies of China's consumer market. It not only gives us a clear picture of China's consumer today but points to an exciting and surprising picture in the future."

Mark Mobius

President, Templeton Emerging Markets Fund, Inc.

"China's economy is increasingly driven by its internal market and its consumers. To succeed in that marketplace it is crucial to stay on top of fast changing consumer needs and tastes. Conghua Li provides invaluable and interesting insights on the most important Chinese consumer trends that are essential for MNCs to understand."
John A Quelch
Sebastian S Kresge Professor of Marketing
Harvard Business School

"This book is a rigorous in-depth study of the Chinese consumer. It is the pioneering research of an insider. It shows what drives consumption in next century's first world economy and how this is likely to evolve creating new opportunities."
Pedro Nueno
Member of the Board, Chairman of the Academic Council
China Europe International Business School (CEIBS)

"Conghua Li is right on target regarding the emergence of a consumer-driven market in China. His timely book is a solid foundation for any marketer contemplating a China launch or expansion. Marketing in China is not for the faint of heart, but absorbing China: The Consumer Revolution will increase your odds for success."
Richard C. Bartlett
Vice-Chairman, Mary Kay Holding Company

Continue on page 247

Chapter 1

The Consumer Revolution

The world's fastest growing consumer society

In October 1996 *CAIFU (Wealth)*, a glossy mainland publication, named Larry Yung as the richest man in China with assets estimated at US$500[1] million. A single individual in communist China with US$500 million? What kind of economy can generate such individual wealth in a nation only two decades removed from Third World privation and isolation?

Deng Xiaoping's return to power in 1978 and the reforms he initiated, from the single-child family to a market-oriented economy, set the wheels in motion. However, it is the consumer, from the farmer in the field to the richest man, that is driving the economic engine forward. It is moving so fast and at such a furious pace that it is expected that China's GDP will surpass that of the United States by the year 2015, even without taking the economic strength of Hong Kong and Macao into consideration. China then will begin to lengthen its lead, with a predicted growth of 8% against 4% or less for the United States.

What does this mean for business strategists wishing to succeed in this economic revolution? The key to marketing success has been shifting rapidly. In the 1970s and early 1980s foreign firms needed good government connections at the national level. Beijing controlled China's international trade. All business activities required the approval of the Ministry of Foreign Trade. By the mid-1980s the key to success shifted to effectively setting up joint venture operations and developing good government relationships at local level. For the second half of the 1990s as well as the future, the most critical factor for market success in China has again shifted to staying on top of the trends of the consumers and the market. Nevertheless, most observers continue to believe *Guanxi* (connections), government access and support, and tax incentives are the most important factors contributing to ultimate success in the China market. These issues have a much lower priority and impact on success than business strategy and overall vision, quality of management, and a product that is carefully tailored to the market. *Guanxi* and government access and support actually fall somewhere between the twenty-first and twenty-fourth out of the 28 most important factors contributing to success, according to a recent survey by the Economist Intelligence Unit. Now, as we approach a new century, business success means keeping up with the changes going on at the consumer level and with a population of 1.2 billion, the implications of those changes are unique not only in scale but in cultural complexity.

Figure 1.1   Critical factors for success in China, 1996

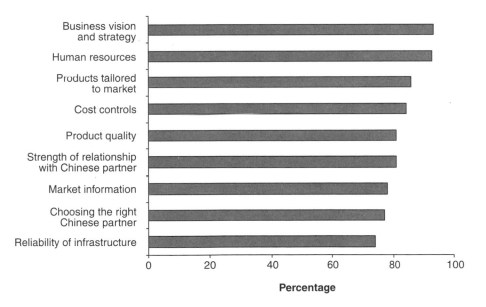

Source: Business China, March 1996. Produced by permission of the Economist Intelligence Unit

This book sets out to analyze China's changing economy at the consumer level. By the year 2000, based on 1995 US dollar value, 450 million people will have annual household incomes in excess of US$3,000. Of these, 100 million will have incomes in excess of US$9,000 which will have a buying power in China equivalent to that of a US$40,000–US$45,000 household income in the United States. The United States might remain the world's greatest military power, but it will be China that dominates the world's economy in the twenty-first century.

Few books have attempted to analyze the economic changes within China from the consumer level. Just as the process of doing business has changed, from ensuring Beijing's approval to today's largely direct business-to-business co-operation, so too has the approach to strategic planning for China changed. Businesses and business strategists must begin to look at the forces driving China's economy from a perspective relevant to these fast-changing times. This means analyzing China's economy and markets at the consumer level, for it is the wants and needs of the consumer in China that is deciding the shape and pace of the nation's economy.

The modern history of China has been shaped as much by famine as by war or conflicting ideologies. Famine in the late-nineteenth century drove many Chinese overseas. Ironically, it is this vast and typically prosperous "Diaspora" of 60 million people worldwide that has helped finance China's economic rebirth. In earlier times, money was sent back to support relatives in the home village. In more recent times, money has flowed back from overseas into an ever broadening variety of foreign invested enterprises.

I was born in China and grew up during the Cultural Revolution. I left China eight years after Mao's death, just as the reforms of Deng Xiaoping began to take effect. I have many relatives in China, some living and working in the cities I visited while doing research for this book. China's transformation is as astonishing to me as it is to everyone else. Astonishing but not entirely surprising if one has some understanding of Chinese history and character.

I spent over 18 months traveling the length and breadth of China to assemble the data for this book. I visited Beijing, Shanghai, Guangzhou, Harbin, Urumqi, Kunming, Chengdu and Dalian, among other far flung cities to gather first-hand accounts from the instigators of China's fast-changing economic revolution. When I left China in the mid-1980s, changes were still being directed from above. Today, economic changes are rising up from street level in a tidal wave of long suppressed entrepreneurial energy and ambition. The Chinese consumer has come of age. Who exactly is the Chinese consumer? To succeed in business in China today, strategists must understand both the cultural and economic imperatives of this enormous and remarkably powerful market.

Consumers seem to buy things for the same reasons everywhere, except in China, where status is culturally nuanced. How status is defined, and how and where it fits into spending patterns is unique and changing. It is unique to regions, as well as to specific categories of consumers. To understand the meaning of status in China today, and how it influences spending, requires some understanding of the nation's social and cultural values.

There are two main reasons for the consumer boom in China today. They are both relatively recent and were instituted by the national government. The first are social changes that began with the single-child family and led to a general shifting of responsibility for personal welfare from the State to the individual. Specific changes include a reduction in the level of State subsidization for housing and pensions, the abolishment of the life-long employment system, a reform of the citizen registration system, and an increase in the cost of education, especially university tuition. However, the most dramatic changes are the economic reforms that have led to a largely free and open market economy.

The government's single-child per family policy has been remark-ably successful in controlling population growth. It has also, almost 20 years later, created a maturing generation of what are sometimes called "little emperors" — children who have been showered with the care, attention and financial means of up to ten adults. This gen-eration has been raised in peaceful, prosperous times and continues to receive, even as they move into adulthood, the financial support of doting parents, grandparents, aunts and uncles.

Though the term "little emperor" has been used widely to describe this generation, it no longer seems appropriate or even descriptive. The first generation of the single-child consumer, or the s-generation, is now entering adulthood and assuming the real life responsibilities. The s-generation is far from little, and far more earth-bound than emperors.

Economic reforms followed on the heels of the single-child family. Significantly, these reforms began on collective farms, in rural regions and not in big city centers. Farmers were allowed to keep and sell for profit, crops they grew on land not allocated strictly for government quotas. Efficiency and productivity rose in relation to profits realized. The success of these policies spread the reforms to all sectors of society. Of course, there were hiccups in the system. At one time, shoe repairmen in city streets were earning three times the monthly wage of a university professor; however, such disparities have been dramatically reduced.

These economic reforms and social changes are largely responsible for China's economic rebirth and growing consumer boom. In following chapters, the more specific social and economic impli-cations of these innovations, in relation to consumer spending, lifestyle and aspirations, will be explored.

Anyone in the West who has read anything about China in the past few years has read astonishing tales of rags to riches. These colorful anecdotes have inspired many foreign companies to move into China.

Many have succeeded; some have suffered false starts or failure. There are many obstacles, and nothing worthwhile is ever easy. This book sets out to explore and discuss the dominant trends in China's consumer market, and offers current facts, figures and analysis in the hope that this information may help guide your China business strategy. The approach is structured to assist those companies wishing to enter China, as well as those already established in China and wishing to expand. It is also relevant to both domestic and international companies. I believe that, for any consumer business, success will only come if business strategy is rooted in a solid understanding of the consumer.

Of course, there are serious challenges. China is going through phenomenal fundamental change. Competition is strong, consumers' demands and the regulatory environment change rapidly, the marketplace itself is complex and difficult to read, and business infrastructure is generally less developed.

Will the reforms be stopped? Will the government stop this high-speed movement toward more modern styles of business and higher standards of living? A rapid transformation of the legal system, significant disparities in regional economic development within China, huge migration of farmers into cities, rapidly rising unemployment, increasing financial and social polarization between the rich and the poor, unforeseeable social consequences of a single-child society, and rising drug, AIDS and crime problems all give rise for concern. Though the process of economic transformation carries considerable risks and challenges, they are not likely to inspire the new generation of leadership to change course. How could they, the new generation is too busy making money. Larry Yung, the richest man in China, is also the son of China's Vice President, Rong Yiren.

Goh Chok Tong, Prime Minister of Singapore, said it best, "The genie is already out of the bottle and cannot be put back. There is sufficient internal dynamism for China to grow robustly even without outside help."

Underlying social and cultural values

China has been closed off from the rest of the world for much of its 5,000-year history. This isolation has reinforced the strength of its underlying social and cultural values and created a nation uniquely confident of its own identity — so confident that outside cultural influences do not compromise China, they become part of China.

Many nations put up barriers to protect their culture. Insecurity leads them to believe that outside influence will weaken their identity. Perhaps it will. But in China, outside influences are embraced, but transformed. Presently, McDonalds is having considerable success with its fast food restaurants in China. Why are they successful? It is not the food, at least not yet. It is the novelty, status and symbol of McDonalds that fuels its present day success. It is the place to be, and be seen. Whether or not it is the place to eat is another issue entirely. Certainly, McDonalds would not be quite so successful if consumers were only being drawn by the food. Chinese consumers have embraced McDonalds, but for their own particular reasons. Competition is fierce. When the crunch comes, will McDonalds know what to do?

In this section the underlying social and cultural values that have shaped the Chinese consumer's habits and tastes will be examined. China's gravitational nature, its tendency to absorb and digest all that enters will also be looked at.

The underlying social and cultural values that most influence Chinese consumers can be broken into four fundamental elements: life extension, interpersonal, social status and assimilation.

Life extension

The desire for a long life and reverence for the elderly and children are characteristics of Chinese culture. Life extension is not only about extending one's own life, it also means a deeply felt connection to ancestors and future generations. It is as if the individual is standing in the middle of an empty field holding onto a long rope suspended at waist level. The rope represents all past and future generations. It begins somewhere too far away to see, and disappears over the horizon. The individual holds onto this rope tightly, for it connects them to their ancestors, and shows the way for future generations. They would never let go of the rope for they would be lost. They only exist because of their place in the continuum between past and future.

The struggle to extend life is not only about wanting your children to carry on your name and preserve your reputation. It is also about passing along to them, the worldly goods you might have accrued so that their journey toward immortality might be easier, and their status higher. Money is consciously put aside for an inheritance. It is not money that might have been used for a vacation, or renovating the house. An inheritance for your children is as fundamental as their education or health. China's per capita rate of savings is one of the highest in the world. There are other more important reasons for high savings, but inheritance plays a significant role.

The family is the prime unit in society. It is within the family that the individual first learns social and cultural values. Of course, the values of the family unit reflect the broader values of the society. The motivations of consumers within the family are sometimes easier to see than in other groups in society because of greater levels of trust. Generally, greater trust leads to greater openness. Reverence for age is expressed by the privileged position of seniors, and aspirations for greater status are expressed in an absolute commitment to the child. It is also clearer in the family than in society that there is often a great deal of "disconnection" between the purchaser and the end user — the person for whom the product or service is ultimately destined. The elderly save their money to pass along to the young as an inheritance. The inheritance prolongs their lives, as it increases the child's status, and if the elderly do spend, they spend on their grandchild. They buy what the grandchild needs, or what they think the grandchild needs. Middle-aged adults are the largest purchasers of health tonics for prolonging or enhancing life, but they are buying largely for their parents, because they believe the tonic will prolong their parents' lives. Young people between 18 and 28 are the greatest consumers of expensive international goods. Not because they have higher salaries than their parents or older colleagues, but because they live at home and their parents cover their basic living costs. There is a more subtle "disconnection" here between purchaser and end user. Parents are purchasing food and household goods for "adults" who have the means to provide for themselves.

Social and cultural values are learned through osmosis and reinforced emotionally through close relationships within the family. Nobody questions why it is a good idea to save for your child's inheritance, they just do it. If there is a rational side to life extension it shows up in a general concern for long-term planning, and a concern for the long-term viability of goods and services expressed in such qualities as durability and value retention. In China, people often speak of planning three steps ahead before taking a first step. Clearly, investment in a child is long-term planning, but so is saving money and a willingness to spend money to develop relationships outside the family that may serve to improve long-term quality of life or status. The disproportionate amount of time and money spent acquiring status only makes sense if status endures and in China, often it does, bringing glory to the family long after the death of the person who worked so hard to achieve it.

Interpersonal

The word "interpersonal" is used throughout this book to describe the strong tendency of the individual to relate to other people or other people's opinion. In China, the individual's identity is always determined by how others view him or her. Often, the interpersonal interaction of the Chinese is confused with "collective" interaction. Interpersonal is a more subtle and independent type of interaction. The individuals measure themselves in the mirror of others' opinion, but do not necessarily work together with others towards a shared vision or goal. The following ancient anecdote points out the dangers and differences of the interpersonal nature of the Chinese.

A monk had to walk a long distance every day to fetch water from a spring. He carried the water home in a bucket. One day he was joined by another monk. The first monk was not prepared to fetch water for the two of them, he wanted the new monk to share the work equally. The monks solved the problem by carrying the bucket on a bamboo pole between them. A third monk arrived. No matter how hard they tried they couldn't find a way to distribute the work evenly among the three of them. No one was prepared to do more than the others. Eventually, they all died of thirst.

If the monks had been interacting more collectively, they would have reached some compromise to ensure collective survival. Sadly, no one was going to step forward and risk suggesting a solution the others might then reject, and no one was prepared to take on any more or less responsibility than any other. The consequences were extreme and tragic but clearly illustrated an aspect of China's interpersonal nature.

Qu Tong Xing is an academic term used to describe the Chinese characteristic of blending in with the crowd. Older generations are expected to wear dark somber clothing. Wearing grey is considered daring. All business people are expected to carry cellular phones. They would be perceived as being unsuccessful or incompetent if they didn't have one. Generally, people follow the tastes of the group. The challenge for marketers is to determine groups — most people belong to several different groups: family, neighborhood, school, work, etc. For our purpose, we call these overlapping planes of influence clusters.

In 1995, one of the world's top ten pharmaceutical companies tried to enter the market using a statistical approach. They felt they could be successful in the China market if only a small percentage of their target market of 300 million took to the product. They went to the streets and promoted their product without focus, to as broad an

Figure 1.2   Clusters model

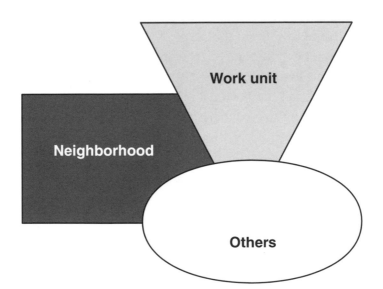

audience as they could find, but sales remained flat. When their approach failed, they switched strategies and focused attention on a specific cluster. The cluster they approached was the Hutong, a residential street, lined on both sides with adjacent courtyards shared by neighboring families. The target audience was smaller, but their contacts more intense. Slowly, the product came to be accepted in the Hutong. One family would try it and tell another family. As momentum reached a critical mass within the Hutong, they then moved to other Hutongs and will eventually move to more public clusters of work, education and leisure groups. Residents of the Hutongs belong to these clusters, their presence will help facilitate the cross-cluster access and entry. Eventually, the product will begin to realize its market potential. This cluster-marketing strategy has already seen company sales quadruple in one year.

An advertising campaign for health tonics targeted exclusively for senior citizens would probably fail. The elderly don't buy the products and so wouldn't pay much attention, no matter how sophisticated the advertising campaign. The middle-aged who buy these products for their aging parents wouldn't see advertising that didn't fall within their fields of interest, or follow their lifestyle. Again, we have an example of the frequent disconnection between purchaser and end user, and the interpersonal nature of life in China. Marketers would have to identify the appropriate interconnecting clusters and design a marketing campaign to reach middle-aged children of aging parents.

The disconnection that often appears between purchaser and end user appears again in the disproportionate amount of money spent on gifts and entertainment to cultivate the *Guanxi* – relationships – with individuals within one's group, especially individuals who might be able to increase one's status — wealth, power or knowledge — within the group. Of course, it also reinforces the importance of the interpersonal relationship generally. Obviously, this is also done to cultivate relationships with individuals from outside of one's specific group, and from a group of higher status or power. Consumers are buying gifts or services for others to enjoy. This happens in the West as well. What is significant here is the generally higher level of commitment of individuals to this system and the higher proportion of the individual's income dedicated to these tokens. Essentially, the gift must reflect the giver's respect towards the recipient's status, not the giver's means. Since many gifts are offered to those of higher rank, the means required to purchase them can be considerable. The consumer rationalizes the expense as a long-term investment. The benefit to the consumer might not be immediate, but developing a relationship with a person of higher rank may eventually lead to advancement.

Renao is a word describing an atmosphere of boisterous celebration. Essentially, it describes the individual's attraction to the crowd. *Renao* can refer to crowds celebrating Chinese New Year in a town square, or friends and family gathered around a table for a meal. *Renao* implies entertaining and entertaining reinforces *Guanxi*. In the West, it's unusual to find a restaurant with tables seating more than four. In China, a table for eight is standard. A table for eight brings good fortune. A *Ba Xian Zhuo* is a traditional square table seating eight, eight places for the eight immortals or celestial beings of Chinese tradition. Every home is expected to have at least one square table seating eight. Often, during my trips through China, I would find myself eating alone. Waiters would ask me how many would be joining me. When I told them I was alone, they always looked at me as if they hadn't quite understood what I'd said. It's unusual for people to eat alone. It's even more unusual if you want to eat alone.

Individuals within a group strive to be different. They want to be the same, but different. If the trend is to wear a name brand tie to work, then everybody wears name brand ties, but the individual tries to make sure his tie is different from everybody else's. Different but the same. No one wants to take responsibility for introducing the name brand as the brand of choice, in part out of fear of rejection and the humiliation that would follow, but once introduced, everyone follows.

Social status

Confucius promoted the notion that everybody had a specific status in society, and that one's conduct should always be informed by their status. If you were the emperor, then rule absolutely. If a minister in the government, then serve the government. If a father, dominate the family, and if a son, "Show up and shut up."

In ancient times, status was codified by the *Ke Ju* system. This was a selection process through imperial exams. The levels can be very loosely compared to university degrees offered in the West: BA, MA and PhD. The exams were strict and rigorous and only those with high enough scores could proceed to the next level. The highest scores led to important positions in the central government. The very top scholar was often married to a daughter of the emperor. It was a merit-based system. The poorest, lowliest child could rise to the top based only on hard work and natural gifts. This system imbued the culture with respect for learning and the importance of hard work. It also offered a clear and rational way of measuring and signifying status within society.

In China today, wealth, power and knowledge are the three defining attributes of status. Wealth is the easiest attribute to measure, but perhaps the hardest to acquire. Becoming truly wealthy often requires equal measures of hard work and luck. Power is hard to quantify, and is more ephemeral and fleeting than wealth. Power can lead to wealth as it can open doors to opportunity that might be closed to others. Knowledge is perhaps the only attribute that remains with the individual no matter what the circumstances of his or her life. Knowledge is the only status-defining door open to all Chinese, of any background or circumstance. It is highly democratic as entrance exams to schools or universities follow municipal or national standards, and the only route to success is personal determination, discipline and intellect. A peasant from a mountain village has as great an opportunity of success as the son of a high-ranking government official.

Families invest heavily in their children's education because it offers the new generation the best opportunity for advancement. They hope their child will go to university; if the child get sent to a university in the West, all the better. An undergraduate university degree contributes very little to individual success in the West. The proliferation of universities and government funding makes it accessible for most of the population. Like anything else, the greater the supply, the lower the value. In 1994, there was space for only 900,000 students in China to enter university and no more than 2,000 of the very best students were sent abroad. Over two million high school graduates competed for the best possible qualification. They suffered through eight exams, spread over four days. The exams covered the basic academic subjects of either the sciences or the humanities and were set to national standards. I studied natural science. To prepare for university entrance exams, I studied all the exams that had been conducted between 1954 and 1964. The pressure to succeed was enormous and the tension during exams almost unbearable. Fortunately, I received a high enough grade to carry on to university. Unfortunately, many brilliant minds, for one reason or another, miss an opportunity for a higher education. For those who succeed, and complete a university degree, the doors of opportunity open.

Parents of the s-generation have costly expectations for their child. Costly for both the parents and the child. On one hand, the children are showered with attention and material goods, and not expected to lift a finger to provide for themselves. On the other hand, they are expected to study late into the night, and are pushed to succeed in a system that even requires entry exams at the middle school level.

Any product or service that clearly expresses status or position will be successful. A cellular phone suggests you're a busy entrepreneur or business professional. A basic cellular phone also costs as much as an average salaried worker's yearly income. If it suggests you're successful, and helps you toward greater success, all the better. All cosmetic consultants of the Mary Kay Corporation — one of the most successful marketers in China — are equipped with an eye-catching pink cellular phone.

Status becomes complicated in interpersonal relations. Gifts are given to commensurate with the status of the recipient, not according to the means of the giver. Obviously, this creates a significant disconnection between the purchaser and the end user. The wealthy, and those with higher incomes, are perhaps not the only significant consumers of luxury items. If marketing campaigns were focused according to income or worth, the message would miss a significant percentage of the consumers of these items. To attract the attention of this group, it would be important to stress the characteristics of the product that were status oriented, as they are being purchased only for how they will reflect or confirm the status of the recipient.

Assimilation

The way of the mean, and action only through consensus, has created a nation that embraces rather than rejects that which is different at beginning. Anything that does not threaten the foundations of the culture or belief systems enters easily. This "gravitational pull" could only have developed in a nation with a strongly entrenched identity and set of cultural values.

Genghis Khan conquered much of China in the Middle Ages but his culture and identity disappeared soon after the collapse of his dynasty. The language and culture of the Manchus was fading even before the end of their reign. In the longer term, China accommodates what it can, transforms what it can't accept to its own needs, and that which is extreme, extraneous, or atypical, is ejected.

Outwardly, China may appear averse to change, but the Chinese are known to enjoy a high degree of risk. Certainly, they're renowned gamblers, but they're also voracious consumers of new products and trends — the "novelty" success of new products in China is short. If a foreign or domestic company wants its products or services to have a long life, it will have to answer more fundamental cultural concerns, be flexible and fast to meet the ever-changing tastes of China's new consumers.

The cigarette market is huge in China. Well-known foreign brands do not command the premium position that many expected. One would assume foreign brands to be more expensive than domestic brands. Marlboro and 555's sell for RMB[2] 15, but among the most popular domestic brands, Zhong Hua's sell for RMB 35 and Yun Yan's sell for RMB 40. Foreign companies cannot assume that they will succeed just because their products have been successful elsewhere, or have the cachet of a famous brand name.

As production in China becomes more sophisticated and absorbs the technology and style of Western products, it begins to claim, or take back, significant domestic market share. A 1996 survey conducted by the State Statistics Bureau showed that for the first time since the economic reforms began, Chinese domestic household electrical appliances now dominate the market. The survey involved 100 large department stores in 35 cities. Chinese brands such as

Changhong televisions, Little Swan washing machines, Rongsheng refrigerators and Glanz microwave ovens now dominate the market. China is one of the few countries in the world where Japanese televisions do not claim a majority of the market share. Imports in many sectors are falling. From 1995 to 1996, the number of air-conditioners imported into China fell 28%, refrigerators fell 27%, video cameras fell 77%, and television imports were down 47%.

In March 1997, the *Asian Wall Street Journal* published a report on current consumer trends. The Lins live in Guangzhou and are a typical couple in their mid-30s. They own all the home appliances they need at the moment. They are sophisticated consumers and can tell if a brand is from a joint venture, an import, or a Chinese brand. They are not at all impressed by the reputations of international brands. Mrs. Lin claims that goods manufactured in Shanghai are as fine as any manufactured anywhere in the world. "I see a lot of the international brands on television, but they do the same thing as local brands; they're just more expensive."

Generally, the degree of risk taken is directly related to the individual's perceived control over outcome. Smaller ticket items have more room for the shock of the new than more expensive items. One area of great variety and change is food. It also offers an example of "internal" assimilation. It is often said in China that the Chinese will eat everything in the sky except planes, everything in the sea except torpedoes, everything on the ground except tanks, and everything under the ground except land mines. In Sichuan province, insects are a much sought after delicacy. Today, these delicacies are increasingly popular across the nation. If China is willing to assimilate foreign goods, why shouldn't it also absorb its own?

The process of assimilation can be a trap for international companies. Initial market success can be deceptive. Companies must remain sensitive to consumers' needs and changing tastes. Presently, Coca Cola and Pepsi sell their products at higher prices than in the

West. A great deal of their success and popularity however, comes from the novelty value of the products. Novelty value eventually wears off, sometimes sooner rather than later. If Coke and Pepsi do not begin to provide additional value of some kind, either their price or market share will surely fall, no matter how strong their marketing and distribution machine may be. Chinese consumers are shrewd and they will assimilate. Foreign goods may whet the appetite and tickle the fancy, but it takes more than novelty value to have long-term success.

The forces shaping future consumption

Social and cultural influences rise up at consumers from great depths. Their origins and rationale are rooted in the distant past, origins too far away to identify precisely. Changes to these influences only appear slowly, over a long period of time. If one were to try and predict a shift in social and cultural influences, it might be said that over the next few decades, the Chinese citizen may make a slight shift from an interpersonal nature to a more individualistic nature with little need to confirm within a group or cluster — not necessarily individualistic in a Western way, but a shift away from seeing himself or herself always identified through the group. Again, the Chinese don't copy cultures, values, styles and behaviors, they make things into their own; they assimilate.

The forces shaping future consumption exist in the here and now. In some cases, this will be the first time such data has been published. Like much of the phenomena described in this book, there is a high degree of interaction between the distinct areas of influence explored. The process began with seemingly small changes in government policy, but market reforms and the single-child family cannot help but have a tremendous impact on a nation of China's size. Some of these changes are now taken for granted — the general improvement of the country's infrastructure, and the international interaction that began more than a decade ago. There are other significant and identifiable forces at work now that will have a significant impact on the direction of future consumption.

Rising economic prosperity

China's gross domestic product (GDP) has grown at a compounded annual rate of 9.5% for the past 19 years. Many of the economic targets set out in China's Eighth Five Year Plan (1991–95) were achieved in only three years, including GDP, international trade, and foreign direct investment (FDI). The government remains optimistic and predicts that the economy will continue to grow at a compounded annual rate of 8% during the Ninth Five Year Plan (1996–2000). International institutions project even healthier growth for the same period. The World Bank estimates annual growth of between 8% and 9% until 2004, the Hong Kong and Shanghai Bank projects annual growth of 10% for the next decade, and Goldman, Sachs & Co. estimates annual growth of 8–10% for the next two decades.

Today, China's GDP is second only to that of the United States in purchasing power parity, an astonishing achievement in a very short period of time. If we follow the logic of these figures, it seems only a matter of time before China becomes the world's largest economy. It is no longer a question of if, but when.

China's international trade increased more than 600% from 1983 to 1995. By March 1997, foreign reserves had reached US$114 billion, not including the US$70 billion of Hong Kong's reserve at 1 July 1997.

Figure 1.3   GDP comparison China vs USA

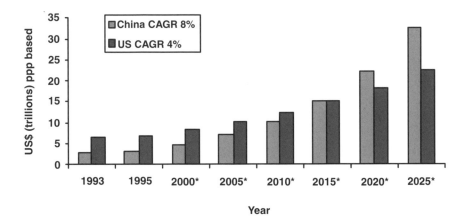

*Estimated figure
Data compiled from: World Bank, analysis of Deloitte Consulting, 1997
Note: CAGR is compounded annual growth rate. The economic strength of
Hong Kong, Macao and Taiwan are excluded in this forecast.
ppp = purchasing price purity

Figure 1.4   China's total international trade

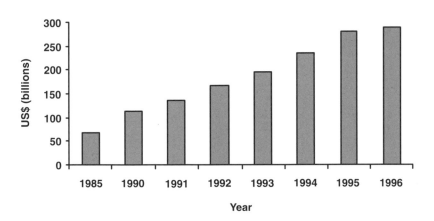

Data compiled from: China Statistical Yearbook, various years

National prosperity is also reflected in increasing levels of personal income. By the end of 1995, there were a total of 600,000 private enterprises registered throughout China with a total registered capital of RMB 260 billion (US$30 billion). Of 600,000 registered companies, more than 30,000 had a registered capital over RMB 1 million each, more than 1,000 had a registered capital of RMB 10 million each, and 20 private enterprises had a registered capital in excess of RMB 100 million each. Average registered capital per enterprise was RMB 437,000.

There were 22.4 million single entrepreneurs registered in China in 1995 with a total registered capital of RMB 147.2 billion. Overall average registered capital per entrepreneur was RMB 6,574. In 1995, average annual income for these entrepreneurs reached RMB 20,000, considerably more than the national average for urban residents of RMB 4,288.

By 1994, the average annual income of employees in the telecom industry had reached RMB 15,639. In another traditionally high-income industry, the airline industry, the average reached RMB 14,912.

Since 1991, 20,000–50,000 international firms set up operations in China each year. Income levels at these firms are 2–4 times the level of State-owned enterprises. In 1996, basic level secretaries at foreign invested enterprises earned an average income of RMB 20,000 per annum. The receptionists at a top US investment bank in Shanghai command salaries as high as RMB 96,000 a year. Today, many local business professionals command monthly salaries in excess of US$4,000.

Average wage earners have seen their incomes increase dramatically in recent years. Between 1978 and 1995 the consumer price level increased 200%, but incomes increased 600%. The increase in income was more dramatic in larger cities. In Beijing, incomes increased an average of 900% between 1978 and 1995. By 1995, there were 150 million people in China with an average annual household income above US$3,000. By the year 2000, the number is expected to grow to 450 million people.

From 1985 to 1994, the national average annual expenditure per consumer increased 150% net of inflation. In urban areas, particularly in larger cities, with greater growth, the increase was even more

Figure 1.5   Urban per capita annual income

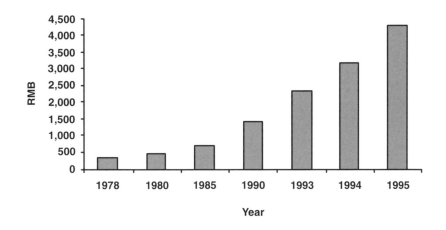

Data compiled from: China Statistical Yearbook, various years

significant. In Beijing, average annual expenditure per consumer increased approximately 180%, in Shanghai increased 160%, and in Guangzhou increased over 200%. These figures cover a broad range of individuals with increasing wealth but give little specific idea of high-end growth. China's millionaire class is growing exponentially. *CAIFU (Wealth)* is dedicated to celebrating the lives and lifestyles of these newly rich. High-end Western consumer goods can now be found in most cities, including remote centers such as Urumqi in

Xinjiang province. There are probably more S-Class Mercedes in Beijing than in any other city in the world. Chic boutiques sell Gucci, Cartier, Chanel and Louis Vuiton. Chinese owned and operated Rolls Royces, Cadillacs and BMWs cruise the streets of Shanghai, Beijing and even Dalian.

Not all wealth is displayed so conspicuously. In fact, income levels of the average worker are significantly higher than figures

Figure 1.6 National total retail market

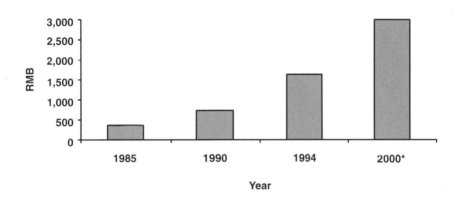

*The estimation for 2000 is based on 1994 RMB
Data compiled from: China Statistical Yearbook, various years, and analysis of Deloitte Consulting, 1996

from State bureaus suggest. Generally, 30% or more of the average worker's income is offered indirectly, and not subject to tax. No accommodation is made for this in income level statistics available from the State. A factory worker may have a declared taxable income of RMB 600 per month, but take-home additional allowances that may bring the actual total to RMB 900.

Many people in China also have second jobs, jobs that often double their gross income, much of these are still conducted in cash,

Figure 1.7   Typically, here's how it's done, 1996

Salaries	RMB	
Skill salary	350	
Job salary	250	
Sub-total	600	(subject to tax if more than RMB 800)
Allowances (cash)		
Transport	10	
Haircut	10	
Medical	60	
Books/newspapers	10	
Inflation	50	
Bonus	50	
Other benefits	110	
Sub-total	300	(not taxed)
Total income	900	

with little or no paper trail. China's national tax system is not yet strong enough, nor sophisticated enough, to accommodate these issues.

The underestimation of average annual income may seem of little significance to readers in the West, but the impact is tremendous for market analysts and business strategists. The income distribution chart (Figure 1.8) shows that an increase of 30% in average household income level would translate into an increase of several hundred percent in market size for some products. Obviously, this kind of discrepancy has a disproportionately large impact on specialized markets such as high-end consumer goods.

Economic prosperity has affected some areas more quickly and profoundly than others. The per capita living space in both urban and rural areas has almost doubled since 1980. The larger the home,

Figure 1.8   Income distribution and impact on purchasing power

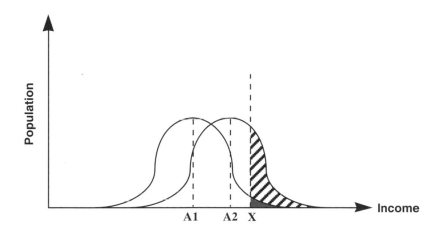

Note: A1 – the statistical mean of income distribution, based on official sta-
         tistics
       A2 – the statistical mean of income distribution, based on estimation
         of real income
       X – the minimum income level to afford certain goods

the more products needed to fill it; and the more the Chinese consumers have, the more they want.

In the 1980s, it was rare to find Chinese guests in three star hotels.
Today in Chengdu, 10–15% of hotel guests in four or five star hotels
are domestic Chinese businesspeople or tourists. Of these domestic
guests, only 10% are having their accommodation paid for by their
employer, or out of business expenses. Today, in three star hotels,
almost all the guests are domestic Chinese.

The rise in income levels has attracted the attention of manufacturers of consumer goods from around the world. Almost all major
brands of consumable can now be found in China. Even the Danish
luxury electronic manufacturer Bang & Olufsen is there. And Bose,
Bang & Olufsen's competitor from the US, is, of course, there.

Figure 1.9   Residential living space in China

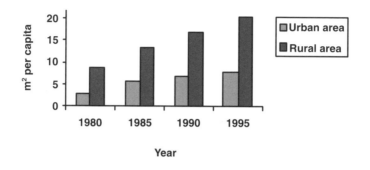

Data compiled from: China Statistical Yearbook, various years

Figure 1.10   Urban residents' ownership of household assets, 1996

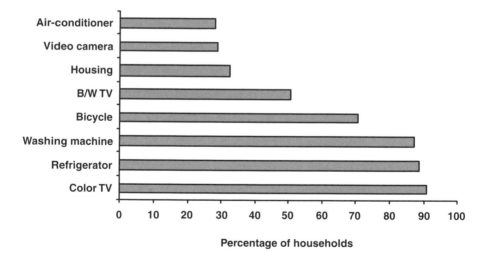

Data compiled from: Zero Point Market Survey and Analysis Ltd Beijing, China, 1996, covering 2,579 families in Beijing, Shanghai, Guangzhou, Chongqing, and Shenyang

International interaction

A new word has entered the Chinese popular vocabulary, *Jie Gui*. It is not really a new word but it has new meaning. The roots of the word are *Jie*, which means "to connect", and *Gui*, which means "train track". Together, the words mean connect, join together, or integrate China with the rest of the world. This term applies to everything from adapting accounting practices to internationally accepted accounting standards, to an internationally compatible legal system, import duties, financial markets, commercial markets, and the observance of international copyright laws on intellectual property.

In the late 1970s, the doors were opened and foreign products and investment flowed in. For many years, more flowed in than went out. *Jie Gui* is an attempt to address the one-sided nature of early East–West exchange, and prepare for the arrival of China's economy on the world stage.

The import of foreign goods into China increased 1,100% between 1978 and 1995. The total foreign investment in China from the time the reforms began until 1983 was US$14.4 billion. By 1995, that sum had risen to US$229.1 billion. By 1995, 234,000 foreign companies had set up business in China. Foreign companies continue to move into China at a rate of 20,000 per year. In 1994, in Beijing alone, the total number of foreign funded companies reached 10,000.

The central government began to develop special "Development Zones" in the late 1970s. These zones offered special incentives for international companies. By 1995, there were over 380 Development Zones spread throughout China. Initially, these zones were located in the coastal region. Today, they are spread throughout China. I met Canadians in Xinjiang province working on an agricultural venture, Israelis in Qinhai province developing natural resources, and Americans participating in high-tech development in the province of Shaanxi.

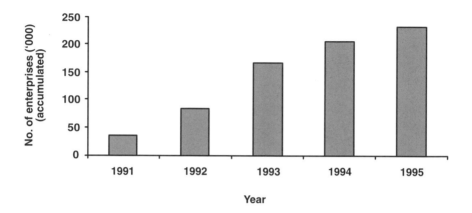

Figure 1.11   Foreign invested enterprises in China

Data compiled from: Statistical Yearbook of China, various years

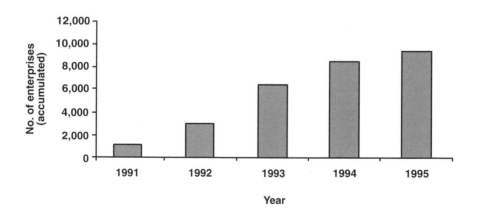

Figure 1.12   Foreign invested enterprises in Beijing

Data compiled from: Statistical Yearbook of China, various years

The number of foreign tourists entering China increased from 5.7 million in 1980, to 46.4 million in 1995. In the late 1970s, foreign tourists rarely ventured beyond the major cities. The growth of the tourist industry has opened China up to the foreign travelers and the influences their presence brings.

Figure 1.13   Number of special Development Zones in China

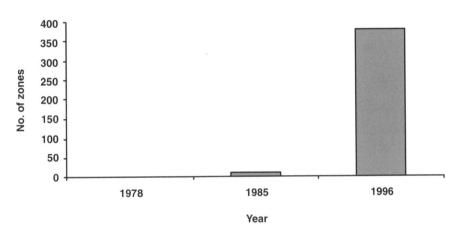

Data compiled from: State Planning Committee, 1996

Foreign tourists, products and ideas have changed China irrevocably. Foreign media penetrates the country, with CNN and Star TV available in many hotel rooms. Millions of children have made Walt Disney's *There Was a Little House* China's most popular radio program. The fashion magazine *Elle* is available in translation, and some of the latest Hollywood movies are released in China shortly after they're released in the United States. *Hurricane*, a recent Hollywood blockbuster, was released in China only months after its release in the United States. Many of the developments rising from the foreign tourist market have now become part of the daily life of most

Figure 1.14   International tourists visiting China

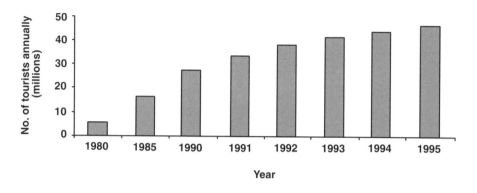

Data compiled from: Statistical Yearbook of China, various years

Chinese. Coffee and a broad range of dairy products have become staples, and bars and cafes are as acceptable as the local restaurants for meeting or entertaining friends or business associates. By the end of 1996, changes to government policy made it easier and faster for Chinese residents to travel abroad. Currently, over six million Chinese business people and tourists travel abroad annually. Clearly, the doors are opened wider and wider, and the exchange of ideas, culture and technology is moving ahead at breakneck speed.

Changing demographics

The policy of one child per family has slowed population growth. Nevertheless, the population of China increases each year, enough to fill a city the size of Shanghai. Every three years the population grows enough to fill a country the size of Canada. China's population is expected to reach 1.4 billion by 2010, and should peak at 1.5 billion around 2025.

China's demographics resemble those of many developed economies. There was a boom in the birth rate during the period of the Cultural Revolution, and another mini-boom in the late 1980s when the government temporarily relaxed the one child per family policy. Today, the birth rate in China is declining, and is lower than that of the United States.

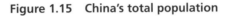

Figure 1.15 China's total population

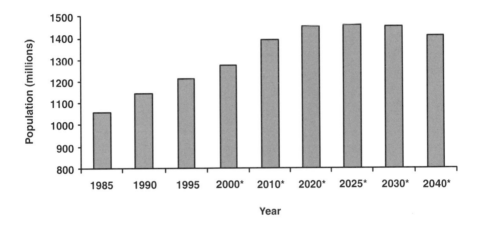

*Estimated figure
Data compiled from: China Statistical Yearbook, Chinese Academy of Social Science, National Planning Committee, China Population Statistics, *Journal of Beijing University*, and analysis of Deloitte Consulting, 1996

One of the most significant demographic changes is China's rapidly growing population of older people. By 1996, the number of people in China older than 60 reached 110 million. By 2000, this figure should jump almost 20% to 130 million. By 2025, one in five people in China will be over 60.

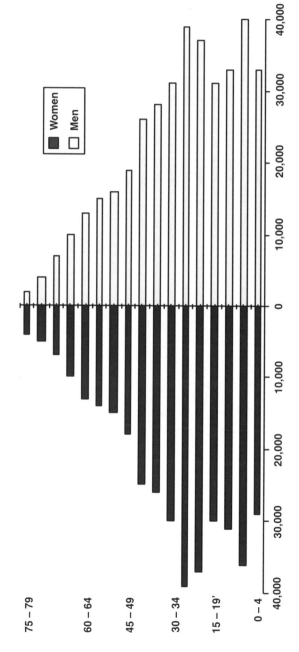

Figure 1.16   China's demographic structure, October 1994, sample size 0.063% of total population

Data compiled from: China Statistical Yearbook, 1995

Perhaps the most profound and interesting demographic issue is the maturing s-generation. In 1996, the first of those children turned 18. This fast maturing group will be China's most active consumers over the next 15 years. As consumers and individuals, they have characteristics unlike any other group.

A significant shift is underway in the structure of Chinese families. Families are becoming smaller and smaller and accommodating fewer and fewer generations. I come from a fairly large family. My mother and father each had four siblings, but none of their marriages, including my parent's, produced more than two children. The average family in China has decreased from 4.6 people in 1980, to 3.8 in 1994. Families of three generations or more now make up less than 20% of the national total.

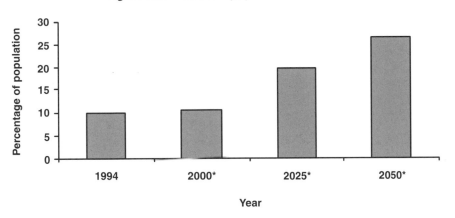

Figure 1.17   The 60+ population in China

*Estimated percentage
Data compiled from: Chinese State Statistics Bureau, Chinese Academy of Social Science, 1995

Figure 1.18   China family structure by numbers of generations, 1994

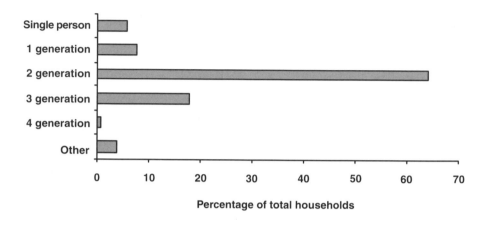

Data compiled from: China Statistical Yearbook, 1995

Figure 1.19   TV ownership in urban China

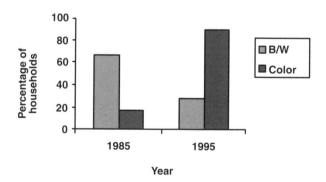

Data compiled from: China Statistical Yearbook, 1996

Infrastructure improvement

Infrastructure improvement falls into three categories. The first deals with electronics and communication, the second with business transaction, and the third deals primarily with transportation.

Since this book is about the consumer, discussion will focus on the product that influences the lifestyle of more consumers than perhaps any other single thing: television. The Ministry of Radio, Film and Television claims that by 1996, television reached 83.4% of the total population of China. MTV, CNN and Star TV are accessible throughout the country and popular with a large audience. Domestic and foreign funded companies are competing for the 2,000 licenses available for commercial and cable broadcasting.

Extensive home ownership of television sets has made television the most important medium for product advertising. Both domestic and international companies compete fiercely for prime time slots which can run hundreds of thousands of dollars for only a few seconds of air time. James Creet, executive media director of Saatchi & Saatchi China was quoted in October 1996 in the *International Herald Tribune* as saying that China still offers the cheapest air time in the world considering the size of the audience. Audience size quickly translates into market size for marketers and business strategists. In 1995, Gallup China conducted a survey that suggests that 92% of the total population watches television, 80% listen to the radio, 70% read newspapers and 66% read magazines.

Cable television is now very common in urban areas. Most families enjoy 10–15 channels from cable service. The cable industry is now entering a second phase of expansion, and is moving into rural areas.

The telephone system is reaching further and further into the lives of the Chinese. Over ten million new lines were installed in the first eight months of 1996. In Guangdong province alone, almost one million lines were installed, and 350,000 cellular phones became opera-

Figure 1.20   TV ownership in rural China

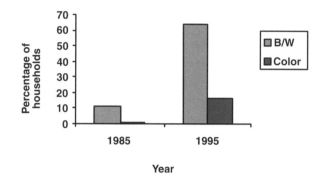

Data compiled from: China Statistical Yearbook, 1996

tional. Telephone installation is not isolated to the more developed or industry rich Pearl River Delta. In the first eight months of 1996, in Jiangsu province, 897,097 telephone lines were installed, in Shangdong province 667,177, in Liaoning province 592,273, and in the city of Shanghai alone, 621,491 lines were installed. By the end of 1996, nation-wide telephone ownership had grown 36% from 4.66% in 1995, to 6.33%. Telephone ownership in rural areas had surpassed 20% nationally.

The quality of telecom infrasystems has been raised by the entry of many international telecom companies. AT&T has been very active in Shanghai, Beijing, Tianjing, Sichuan and many other cities and provinces. Alcatel has done significant work in Yunnan, Sichuan, Guangdong and Shanghai, and Ericsson has won major contracts in Liaoning, Anhui and Guangdong.

As income levels rise, cellular telephones become the phone of choice for many. By the end of 1995, China had become the sixth largest market in the world for cellular phones. In the first eight months of 1996, the number of cellular phones in China increased

Figure 1.21   How much time did you spend yesterday on ..., 1995

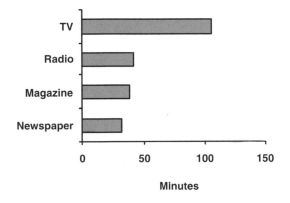

Data compiled from: Gallup China

Figure 1.22   What did you see, listen, or read, yesterday?, 1995

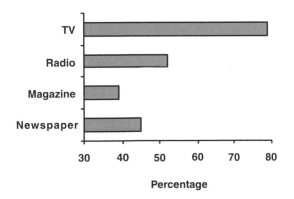

Data compiled from: Gallup China

more than 50%, from 3.6 million to 5.6 million. Equipment costs for cellular phones are 20–100 times that of corded phones, and 3–6 times the overall cost including installation or hook-up. In 1996, China's Global System of Mobile Communication digital cellular network (GSM) had a 16% share of cellular phones. GSM network allows phone users to be connected to many regions. By 2000, that figure should reach 71%.

Over the past decade, telecommunication traffic volume has been growing at 50% per annum as many local and provincial governments recognize the importance of telecommunications in attracting investment and industry. Volume is also increasing due to greater private consumer use. Nationally, China is planning to lay an additional 100,000 km of optical cable by 2000.

By the end of August 1996, there were nearly 20,000 Internet accounts in China. The Internet is available in all provinces and usage is expected to grow at a rate of 400% per year up to 2000. By late 1996, the government lifted curbs on Western media sites on the Internet, and allowed the public to set up their own Internet accounts. Though there are still some restrictions against pornography and sensitive political issues, any citizen can now set up their own Internet account at a major post office, or specialized Internet service provider. In Shanghai, the first private access Internet provider was set up on 4 October 1996. Called the Internet Café, it offers access to the Internet at RMB 50 per hour. Internet accounts are growing at 15% per month and are quickly out-pacing the growth of the existing telecommunications infrastructure.

The infrastructure for business transactions has improved tremendously in China. In 1985, the Bank of China issued its first credit card, the Great Wall Card. By 1987, the Bank of China had become a member of Visa International and began issuing international credit cards in 1988. By the middle of 1996, there were over four million Great Wall Cards in circulation in China.

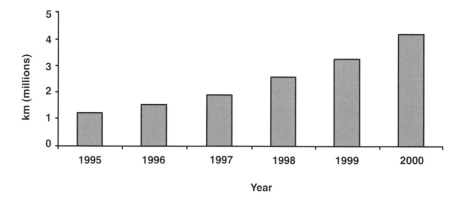

Figure 1.23 Projected demand for optical fibers in China

Data compiled from: Chinese Post and Telecommunication Industrial Corporation, 1995

The government supports the development of the credit card system in China as it will reduce the amount of cash in circulation, and reduce the amount of cash trading. In fact, the government's expressed goal is to see 200 million credit cards in circulation by the year 2000. Dozens of banks in China are issuing credit cards and by the end of 1996, cards in circulation reached 16 million.

Mastercard International is now accepted in 144,000 department stores in China. China is Mastercard's largest market after the United States. Mastercard expects the China market to grow 50% per annum to the year 2000. A joint venture between the Bank of China and Visa International has led to the installation of 260,000 ATMs throughout China. By 1995, ATM use in China had already reached 2.16 per 10,000 people. Use continues to expand dramatically and will soon approach Germany's rate of 3.07 per 10,000 people.

Cash used to be the only means of payment for private individuals. Cheques were the reserve of State offices or companies. Today, with the rise in income levels and increased purchasing power, Chinese consumers need more and more practical personal financial services. In the late 1980s, the Chinese Bank of Industry and Commerce in Shanghai issued the first personal cheques. Personal cheques not only allow consumers a safe and easy means of conducting personal business, they also offer the added feature of paying with your name and signature. The personalized payment has become an expression of confidence and power. A Mont Blanc pen and a book of "Gold Plated" cheques is one of the most popular status symbols today in China.

In July 1993, the Bank of China made personal cheques available in one of its branches in Guangzhou. Three months later, 1,884 chequing accounts had already been opened with deposits totaling RMB 49 million.

In the first half of 1996, the Construction Bank of China began to make loans available to the general public for the purchase of private homes. Other banks have followed suit, making home ownership within reach of countless millions.

Figure 1.24   China's annual investment in road transportation

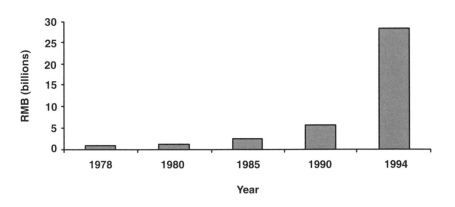

Data compiled from: China's Yearbook of Transportation & Communications, various years

National and regional governments recognize that prosperity will only go where there are roads to carry it, airplanes to fly it, or ports to receive or ship it. The Bazhong region in Sichuan province sits in the Daba mountain range. The region is resource rich but poor and isolated. In 1993, four counties in the region, Bazhong, Tongjiang, Nanjiang and Bingchang, combined their resources to build a 430 km road through the region. The cost was RMB 350 million, but reduced the cost of goods coming into the region by 10%. It also reduced travel time by 50–80%, but increased the number of people traveling through the region by 177%, and increased the overall amount of goods entering the region by 53%. Nationally, railway freight capacity, 1.2 billion tons in 1994, is expected to reach 1.8 billion tons by the year 2000, and an additional 70,000 km of new track will be laid.

China's first high speed train system began operations on 1 October 1996. At 160 km per hour, travel between Nanjing and Shanghai takes only half as long as it used to. Three more high-speed routes will open by 2000: Beijing-Harbin, Shanghai-Beijing and Beijing-Guangzhou.

From 1978 to 1995, the national road system in China increased 24%, growing from 890,000 to 1.1 million km. The road system now links 97% of the nation's towns and cities, and 78% of its villages.

Superhighway construction has been developing rapidly. By the end of 1996, superhighway routes linked many of the major cities in the country including Shenzhen-Guangzhou, Shanghai-Nanjing, Beijing-Tianjin and Dalian-Shenyang. In 1996 alone, over 1,100 km of superhighway were completed in China.

In 1995, nine new airports were opened in China. By 2000, another 41 will have been completed. China's air passenger freight capacity will increase 100% to 90 million by 2000.

Government policy

Changes in government policy that have the greatest impact on consumers' lives fall into two categories: social and economic.

Significant social changes include increasing social mobility, and a shifting of responsibility for citizens' welfare from the State to the individual. For 40 years, a registration system called Hukou, controlled the movement of all Chinese citizens. The Hukou system separated urban, rural, agricultural and non-agricultural residents. If you were classified as a farmer, you could never become an urban resident, and not even move out of your given location. Many called the Hukou system one of the last obstacles in the way of a true market economy. The government has decided to loosen its control over the population moving from region to region. This has created a sea of 100 million migrant workers. Some are highly skilled professionals in search of greater opportunities, many more are unskilled and anxious to find a foothold in China's new economy.

On 1 July 1996, a new Hukou system was put in place to replace the previous one. Under the new system, urban and rural residents are classified according to their current place of residence. Agricultural and non-agricultural residents are separated by current profession. It will take five years to complete the re-classification of the total population. Ultimately, this new system will give a clearer picture of China's population breakdown. It will also allow people with a permanent job and place of residence to gain legal status for their position and claim all the benefits to which residents of the area may be entitled to, particularly in towns and smaller cities across the country. This will further promote the social mobility of the Chinese people. Today, if you can pay the fare, you can travel almost anywhere.

State enterprises have also been affected by the economic reforms. The guarantee of full lifetime employment is also fading quickly as market forces batter the old, inefficient State enterprises. In 1986, employees joining State enterprises began to be engaged under contract. By March of 1996, the guarantee of employment for life had collapsed under the pressure of the new market system and 94 million State employees, or 87% of the total number of employees, had been converted to contract workers. The government compensated State employees for this loss of security by freeing up residency restrictions and encouraging employees to transfer to jobs they might be better suited for. For many, the change brought only insecurity and anxiety, for others it meant opportunity and the possibility of advancement.

Some of these changes are being introduced slowly, allowing citizens to find other means of support. The State has been reducing housing subsidies to State employees, and increasing rent. Because of this, and changing banking practices, more and more people are moving into homes of their own. The residential housing industry, and all industries related to the outfitting or upgrading of housing, are experiencing a boom that is likely to continue well into the next century. As consumers work harder, make more money, and become increasingly sophisticated, they begin to ask for more from limited State social systems, and look elsewhere for additional support and care. Life and health insurance is a growing industry and the over the counter (OTC) pharmaceuticals market, though not yet formally structured and supervised, is booming. Consumers now look for pension plans, health care protection, long-term savings and investment plans. As income rises, and the government withdraws further from the daily lives of its citizens, the polarization between the rich and the poor becomes greater.

The reforms began with agriculture. Recently, the central government shifted even greater priority onto the development of the agriculture sector. It has raised the price of agricultural products and promoted modern production methods. As a result, rural consumers are becoming a significant consumer force, often enjoying higher

Figure 1.25   Market price of agricultural produce in China

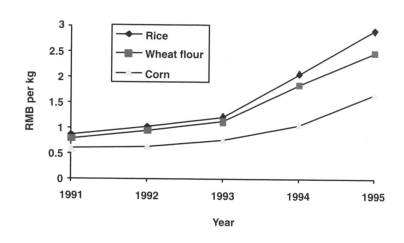

Data complied from: Agricultural Development of China, 1996

levels of disposable income than their urban counterparts. The total inflow of foreign capital for agricultural ventures in Guangdong province between 1993 and 1995 is the same amount as the total amount that was invested in agricultural ventures in the region between 1978 and 1992.

The government is also focusing on developing the nation's more isolated regions, and its untapped natural resources. All efforts are made by local or national government bodies to increase the flow of foreign investment and broaden the base of its contact with China's many emerging industries. Investment has been shifting inland from the Pearl River Delta region and China's traditional coastal economy. This shift of economic development to the western resource-rich regions of China will lead to the creation of even more dynamic new consumer centers.

The government is also further developing the coastal region and hoping development will move to Bohai Bay and transform that

Figure 1.26 China's industry output structure by ownership, 1995

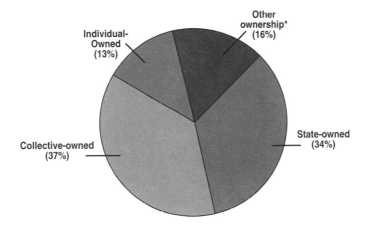

*Foreign investment, private and other companies
Data compiled from: China Statistical Yearbook, 1996

Figure 1.27 The nominal growth rate of China's industry output growth by ownership, 1985–95

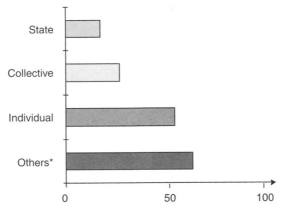

CAGR (%)

*Foreign investment, private and other companies
Note: CAGR refers to compounded annual growth rate
Data compiled from: China Statistical Yearbook, 1996

region into another Pearl River Delta. In coastal regions, much of the economy is shifting to technology-based development. By 1995, there were some 52 high-tech Development Zones in China, most located in the coastal region. The old system of a planned economy has given way to a government trying to keep up with an economy moving ahead at breakneck speed.

Endnotes

[1] By August of 1997, Larry Yung's net worth had shot up to an estimated US$1.3 billion.

[2] 1996/1997 currency of P.R. China: RMB 1.00 – US$0.12 or US$1.00 = RMB 8.30.

Chapter 2

Generations Apart

New wave consumers

China's economic reforms have transformed a nation and created an economic boom unlike any other in the twentieth century. It has all happened in less than 20 years, and presents phenomena that cannot be held up for comparison beside any other similar social or economic change. The interpretation of consumers' motivation and the prediction of future trends presented in this book is the result of an integration of first-hand observations, a careful analysis of the underlying social and cultural background, economic, demographic and regulatory forces and the most current available data.

China's most dynamic consumers are made up of three separate groups. They are differentiated by age and generation. For all three, the availability of consumer goods and services is a relatively new phenomenon. The s-generation has become accustomed to having newer choices every day; young and middle-aged rural consumers are quickly moving toward modernization; and consumers over the age of 60 now look forward to a rich and rewarding retirement.

The s-generation is perhaps easiest to analyze, and probably more predictable psychologically, than their parent's generation and the generation before. Their lives have been stable and consistent, and marked by economic prosperity and rising expectations. They have been conditioned by this experience and their character is unlike any other young generation at any time in this century. The closest parallel that can be drawn would be the baby boomers in North America of the early 1950s, a time of similar prosperity and rising expectations. However, greater expectations fall on the shoulders of the s-generation as many adults look to them for fulfillment of their dreams and family aspirations. The parents of the s-generation are more psychologically complex, as they have experienced economic hardship and watched the reforms and subsequent economic developments with a combination of enthusiasm and confusion. Where is the economy heading? What does it mean to me and my family? The older generation, the 60+ consumers, are perhaps the most conservative and cautious, a psychology shaped by the experience of war, their age, and the skepticism of those who have lived long, seen much and suffered.

The s-generation comes of age

Today in China, the most dominant consumer segment is the population of 18–35 year olds. This segment will soon be replaced by a different kind of young consumer, with a completely different background and outlook. The s-generation has been showered with all the material goods their parents, grandparents, aunts and uncles could find. The first wave of the s-generation is now turning 18. They are as old as the market reforms that have created the economic boom, and will soon become the most dominant consumer segment in China. They do not know what came before and do not care. Materially, they are spoilt. They want for nothing and are insatiable consumers of all the latest fads; but material excess comes with a heavy price.

They are expected to excel at school and are pushed by parents and grandparents up the ladder towards a university degree, in part because of China's now rapid conversion to an increasingly knowledge- and technology-based society. They study late into the night six or seven nights a week. It is an exhausting life that leaves very little free time. Middle schools, high schools and universities all have entrance exams. Standards are high and space limited. Competition for admittance is fierce.

The high expectations of the parents have deep cultural roots.

Status drives their actions, as does life extension. They dress their child in the latest fashions to help them be popular. They encourage them to succeed at school and carry onto university so they might bring honor to the family. How important are these issues? A 1992 survey of 360 urban families in Beijing indicated that an average of 66.3% of total monthly expenditures was dedicated to the single child. Nationally, for urban families, 50–70% of total monthly expenditures are dedicated to the single child. It is highly unlikely the s-generation is going to lose its taste for such high levels of consumption anytime soon. The significance of the high dedication of household expenditure on a single child lies more in its impact on the child's psychology and future consumption behavior than in its impact in a purely monetary sense. For today, it suggests that the actual spending level, direct or indirect, of consumer goods for the young is disproportionate to income or sector size. For the future, it suggests a generation with a strong drive towards a disproportionately high personal consumption level.

In 1995, there were over 427 million children in China under the age of 18. Of this number, 100 million were urban children. It is safe to say that over 90% of these urban children are the single child or s-generation of a family. Following these facts, and for the purposes of this book, it's reasonable to say that there are probably 90 million urban s-generation children, a number greater than the total population of Great Britain, Germany, France, or Italy, and three times the population of Canada. There are also close to 200 million rural s-generations, many of whom will become urban because of the expanding consumer centers (to be discussed in Chapter 3). These children have two parents, four grandparents and assorted aunts and uncles spending disproportionate amount of personal income on them. They spend this money directly on toys, entertainment, clothing, books and stationery, and indirectly by giving the child monthly pocket money that averages RMB 200–300. These 90 million urban s-generation have known nothing but peace and prosperity. They are the center of their universe and they have come to expect their every desire to be satisfied. This group of maturing consumers will be the most active segment of the consumer market during the next 15 years. What will be this segment's characteristics? The first characteristic will surely be the unsatisfiable level of demand. These consumers are accustomed to having what they want whenever they want it. Second, they will be extremely sophisticated consumers. They will know what is available anywhere in the world and how much it should cost. Perhaps more significantly, they will be highly enthusiastic and experienced shoppers. Finally, these consumers will have an extremely broad range of interests. They are a television generation, and as media savvy as any consumer segment in the world. They are also generally more mature than earlier generations as they have interacted more with adults than with other children.

Figure 2.1   How much do you like to shop?, 1996

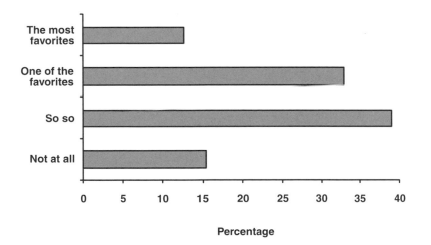

Source: Zero Point Market Survey and Analysis Ltd, Beijing, 1996

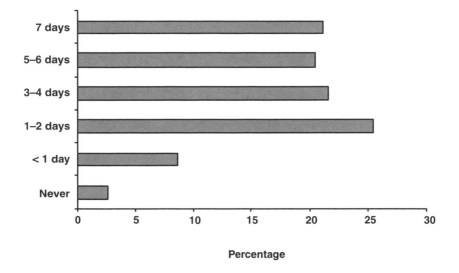

Figure 2.2   How many days a week do you go shopping?, 1996

Percentage

Data compiled from: Zero Point Market Survey and Analysis Ltd, Beijing, 1996

Consumption has always been a part of the s-generation's lives and will be as much a part of their future as it ever was for the baby boomers of the 1950s, but China's s-generation may be even more egocentric in focus, and fickle in its tastes. They will be quick to react, difficult to predict and challenging to satisfy, but they will be the most powerful force in the marketplace. They will be the best educated generation in China's history and the highest earners and the choices they make will have an impact directly and indirectly on every other consumer group in China.

The s-generation is the first generation in China raised in front of a television. They know the language and power of television and respond quickly to effective advertising. Recently, Nabisco Foods China Ltd. ran an ad on television for a new cookie they had developed. The cookie is called Guilian Do Do, which means the funny face of the little Ghost Do Do. The cookie proved to be a huge success and the commercial was so popular that within three weeks of its first appearance, it was being sung by children in the streets of several major cities.

Television has introduced advertising and the outside world. It shows the viewers what they do not have, and by implication what they should come to expect.

Figure 2.3   Future spending behavior by today's age group

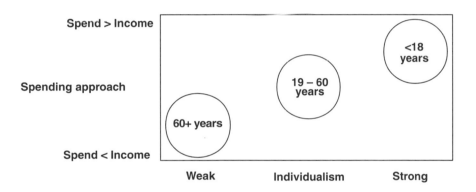

The s-generation is accustomed to spending large sums on themselves. It is not uncommon for them to ask their parents to spend 10% of their total monthly income on one coveted piece of clothing, or a fancy school bag. Today, the money comes from parents, grandparents, aunts and uncles, but as the s-generation mature the challenge will be for them to make enough money to continue these spending habits. Certainly, this generation will spend disproportionately large sums on themselves. As a result, China will begin to move away from a society where people spend money on other's needs, to one with more self-focused spending patterns.

The s-generation will also expect a very high correlation to exist between the work they do and the reward they receive. Recently my cousin, a journalist in Beijing, told me about a five-year old girl who had asked her mother to begin paying her for the chores she did. Another story appeared in the newspaper about a girl from a middle school who stole RMB 500 from her father and spent it all in one night at a dance club with her friends. She was terrified of what her parents would do when they found out and had called one of Beijing's teenage hot lines to ask for advice. Another dispiriting example of this "me" generation is the case of a 13-year-old boy who took the RMB 1,000 his parents and relatives had given him as a birthday gift, to a night club in the South and asked the manager to bring him a female escort to help "celebrate" his birthday. China has rarely seen this type of behavior; however to the s-generation, almost everything seems possible.

Certainly, some of the children from this generation lack solid values, but many more are, for good or bad, just individuals with different values. David is my 16-year-old cousin. He lives in Kunming, in the Southwest of China, with his parents and is rather typical of the maturing s-generation. I have never met anyone of any age in the West so concerned with how he looks as David. He wears casual clothes that are impeccably clean and neatly pressed. He looks like a young investment banker at a weekend training retreat at a four star country resort. He explains that what he wears is standard at his school and that he is far from the best dressed. He was wearing a brown pullover over brown trousers and black leather shoes. The creases in his pants were sharp and his shoes polished. He was particularly proud of his pullover because of the design around the collar. His hair was cut in a contemporary style common in the West.

His father explained of how when they had come upon the pants David was now wearing, David had grabbed them on the display counter and would not budge until his father paid for them. His father seemed almost proud of David's single-mindedness. David's parents both work at State-run enterprises and each makes about RMB 900 per month. I sensed the pride David's parents felt in his confidence. They did not possess the same confidence and single-mindedness themselves, and were very cautious to avoid any overtly critical statements. David, on the other hand, told it like it was. He was almost brash. He was not going to be manipulated and would never accept anything but the best. Finally, David seemed much like any cocky North American teenager. Clearly, this is a focused, determined, and utterly unique generation, and they are being carried forward into the future at great speed by each family's dreams and aspirations.

What of their own dreams? What sort of world will these children make? A survey of 400 urban children aged 7–12 showed that 81.3% dreamed of international travel, 61.9% wanted space travel, 60.2% wanted to be more beautiful or handsome, and almost 90% wanted to be more intelligent (Figure 2.4).

The dreams and aspirations of the s-generation may seem much like those of young people everywhere. The difference is how they and their parents address these aspirations. In North America, young people use personal computers to play games or surf the Internet, in China, a PC is seen almost exclusively as a means of intellectual enrichment and academic advancement. There is a huge market in China for tonics and special foods that parents buy to enhance or enrich their child's intelligence.

The first wave of the s-generation is now entering the job market or university. Soon, they will marry and have children of their own. Daily living had been made easy by doting parents and grand-parents. How will the new couple cope? How will they take care of themselves, never mind each other and a child.

There is likely to be a splintering of the family structure as the first wave of the s-generation begins to have children of their own.

Figure 2.4   What do you dream of doing or becoming?, 1996

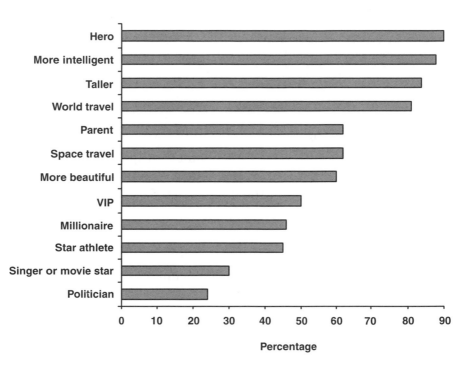

Data compiled from: Zero Point Market Survey and Analysis Ltd, Beijing, 1996

The s-generation will not be able to rely on their parents for child care as their parents will still be in their prime earning years (50–65) and hard at work, and the s-generation will be too busy themselves struggling to establish careers of their own to care for their child as they were cared for. The s-generation will not be able to give the care and attention traditionally reserved for the older generation. This splintering will lead to an increase in both child-care facilities and nursing care for the elderly. Financially, this sector may have the means for such out-of-home support systems, the question is in what way they may or may not accommodate such profound changes to the family environment. There will most likely be an increase in the number of double-income-no-kids (DINKS) families as the s-generation moves into adulthood.

Young and middle aged rural consumers

The reasons for focusing on the s-generation are quite obvious. They are a new social phenomenon and unique in history, and over the next 10–15 years they will have the best education, the greatest opportunities and the highest incomes. But why focus on young and middle-aged rural consumers?

Business strategists tend to believe rural consumers are without the income or the inclination to purchase modern consumer goods. They make the mistake of focusing their attention only on China's 70 million urban consumers living in the 32 cities spread throughout China with urban populations in excess of one million. Certainly, this is a group with growing incomes and easy access to commercial distribution systems, there are some 200 million rural consumers with per capita incomes equal to, or in excess of, urban dwellers. Generally, these rural consumers live in thriving regions such as the Pearl River Delta, the Yangzi River Delta, in pockets around the major cities, in more developed regions along the coast, and along the length of the Yangzi River. The commercial distribution system may be concentrated in the large cities, but it is the rural consumer in outlying areas that makes up the majority of the market. Of course, their dominance will vary from product to product and be relevant to age, income and specific needs.

Most observers believe that over 75% of China's total population is agricultural. In fact, farmers and their families constitute only 45% of China's total population. One-third of China's rural population has either joined collective enterprises, or moved into cities and joined the ranks of China's 100 million migrant workers and family members. The life of this population is closer to that of urban residents than that of farmers. As a result, the rural market in China has a strong urban component. It is becoming an increasingly important consumption market with rapidly rising purchasing power and sophisticated tastes and needs for consumer goods and services.

It is also important to remember that the market reforms that have led to China's economic boom began in the countryside. Many of the farmers who were the early pioneers of economic reform,

Figure 2.5   China's population structure, 1996 (total 1,230 million)

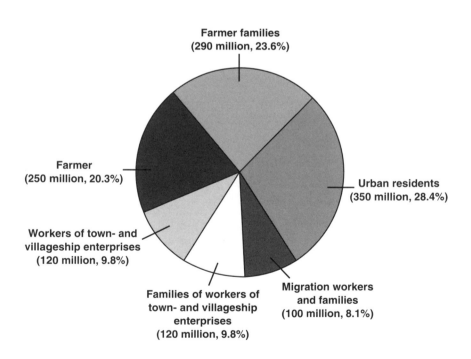

Data compiled from: China Population Statistics, Chinese Academy of Social Science, and analysis of Deloitte Consulting, 1997

especially those living around major cities such as Shanghai, Guangzhou and down the southern coast of China including Zhejiang and Jiangsu provinces, are richer than their urban counterparts.

Total residential construction in rural China was three times higher in rural areas than urban areas between 1986 and 1995. During that period, total urban residential construction was 2.4 billion m^2 against 7.2 billion m^2 total rural residential construction.

As the economy developed and farmers' incomes increased, they shifted from being relatively self-sufficient to more and more dependent on products and services from the marketplace. By 1993, the majority of rural residents' necessities came from the marketplace.

Figure 2.6 Goods purchased by rural residents, 1993

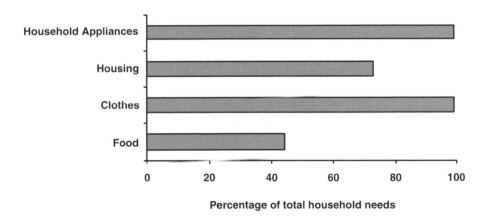

Percentage of total household needs

Data compiled from: State Statistics Bureau of China, 1993

Between 1995 and 1996, per capita income for urban residents grew 3.4% net of inflation. However, rural residents saw their income rise 10% net of inflation during the same period. When purchasing power is added to these figures, the actual worth of disposable income is higher still.

Another significant factor in the importance of young and middle-aged rural consumers is the purchasing value of their money. In 1978, when market reforms began, the purchasing power of RMB 1 in the hands of a rural resident was roughly equivalent to RMB 1 in the hands of an urban resident. Since 1978, the relative purchasing power of RMB 1 in the hands of a rural resident has grown 10–15% higher than RMB 1 in the hands of an urban resident. Official statistics note that income levels for rural residents are lower than those of urban residents. When purchasing power is factored in, the disparity declines considerably. One of the measures of inflation in China is the rise in food prices. Rural residents are generally more self-sufficient than urban residents. They have better access to cheaper food and shelter. If all of these factors are brought into the discussion it soon becomes clear that the average disposable income of some 200 million rural residents is every bit as great or greater than their urban counterparts. Recently, the *Legal Daily* published a story that clearly illustrates this point. A farmer in Shandong province raised chickens, ducks and fish. Total annual household income had averaged RMB 20,000 for several years, but the total annual expenditure of the family of three was never more than RMB 2,000. Purchasing power, rate of inflation, and general self-sufficiency have left this family, and many others, with up to 80% of their total annual income for consumer items, investment, or savings.

The purchasing power of rural consumers was most apparent in a 1995 survey. In Beijing, 12.93% of rural residents[1] owned motorcycles but only 2.4% of urban residents owned motorcycles. In Shanghai, statistics showed similar disparities in favor of rural residents with 22.17% of rural residents owning motorcycles compared to only 0.8% of its urban residents. The disparity in the ownership of sewing machines was not as great with 68% of Beijing's rural residents against 65% of urban residents. In Shanghai, 83% of rural residents have sewing machines against 73% of urban residents. There are many good reasons for the ownership rate of urban residents to be lower than that of rural residents. Nevertheless, the considerable ownership of many durable goods by rural residents shows that they are a formidable and no longer negligible consumer force.

Figure 2.7 Household goods owned by Shanghai farmers, 1995

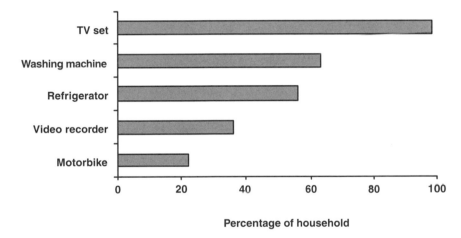

Data compiled from: China Statistical Yearbook, 1996

For our purposes here the rural consumers will be broken down into four categories. First are those involved in agriculture in the countryside, second are those involved in agriculture surrounding large urban centers, third are those involved in the 25 million collective enterprises scattered throughout China, and finally are the rural residents who have migrated from countryside to cities.

More and more people have been moving from the countryside to urban areas in search of greater economic prosperity, and more rural areas are being urbanized. By 2000, almost 60% of China's population will live an essential urban life.

The government offers agri-tech training courses to help farmers keep up-to-date with modern methods and standards. Recently, in Xinjiang province, I attended a lecture organized by a women's committee. Of course it was full, as are all such courses. The lecture had been arranged by a women's committee and only women farmers were invited to attend. However, many young and middle-aged male farmers from the surrounding area invited themselves and stood quietly at the entrance to the hall listening. In rural China men traditionally have a strong chauvinist attitude towards women and are not willing to mix with women's activities. However, learning how to improve agriculture productivity has become so popular that many men have thrown away old attitudes and are learning together with women. The more they learn, the more productive they become and the more prosperous they will be.

In Liujiao county in Shangdong province, a six-person agri-tech training group was sent to help the farmers in the county improve production. From 1994 to 1995, they helped the farmers develop and run 6,000 greenhouses. The average annual income of these farmers increased immediately from 100 to 250%, with many achieving an average per capita annual income of RMB 5,000, which is 20% higher than the average per capita income for urban areas in China. Due to their self-sufficiency, particularly in food, and as the price level in the area is generally low, RMB 5,000 has the purchasing power of a per capita income of RMB 7,000–8,000 in an urban area.

Liujiao county, like many other similar counties throughout China, has not been satisfied with simply increasing production. They have shifted production from low value added basic crops such as rice, to a broader range of higher value added produce generating higher revenues. Profits finance technology, and technology enables them to produce more complicated crops more efficiently. In an effort to pursue even more of the profits available along the food chain, local farmers have constructed a factory for processing food and set up a distribution system to get the products to market. Market reforms began in these areas as modest experiments. Today, they employ cutting edge technology and continue to bring their citizens higher average annual incomes than their urban counterparts.

Figure 2.8   China's meat production

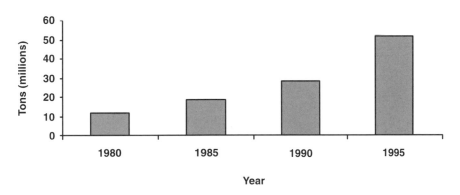

Data compiled from: Agricultural Development Report of China, 1996

Farmers in areas surrounding large urban centers have the benefit of a more efficient and accessible distribution system, and a market close enough to make processing or preserving of fresh produce unnecessary. In 1996, a survey of the rural areas around Shanghai showed that over 700 different vegetables were grown in the region covering five categories and 88 sub-groupings. There are 294 open air seed production sites and over 70,000 greenhouses in the region. Farmers in the area surrounding Shanghai enjoy incomes higher than their urban clients.

As infrastructure improves and technology allows farmers to generate more and more produce, they begin to search for markets beyond their specific region. The rural region around Zhanjiang city in Guangdong province now supplies produce to over 130 cities in China. The total agricultural land surrounding Zhanjiang covers 100,000 acres and generates a total of 650,000 tons of produce with a total value of over RMB 1.2 billion annually.

Many rural residents have experienced a considerable increase in personal income levels in recent years. As a result, many residents living in rural areas around large cities decided to remain in agriculture rather than move to urban centers. In 1995, only 4.1% of rural workers living outside Shanghai expressed an interest in moving to the city in search of greater prosperity.

Collective enterprises are a major force in China's rural economy. There are approximately 25 million collectives in China and they are responsible for 25% of China's total GDP. In 1994, collective enterprises employed over 120 million, representing one-quarter of the total rural workforce. In 1994, these enterprises produced 69.4% of China's total rural GDP, and made up 33.14% of China's total collected income tax. In 1986, they made up 9.2% of China's total exports. By 1994, exports from collectives had risen to 33%. In 1995, exports from collectives reached 40% of China's total exports. The number of people employed by rural collectives is expected to rise to 150 million by the year 2000.

The total output value of collective enterprises in Hainan province reached US$1.4 billion in 1995. From 1995 to 1996 output increased a staggering 40%. Most of this increase is due to improved agriculture production and tourism. The collective enterprises in the province were made up of 1,600 agricultural enterprises. Of the agricultural enterprises, there were ten pig farms raising 10,000 pigs at a time and ten fruit farms with a total of 670 hectares in use. Other collective enterprises in the province include 200 natural rubber enterprises and three tropical fruit juice factories. There are also a number of township tourist enterprises handling approximately one million tourists each year.

Figure 2.9   China's fruit production

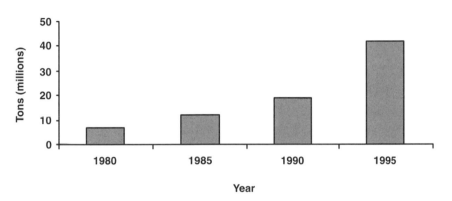

Data compiled from: Agricultural Development Report of China, 1996

As rural areas generated wealth, they begin to direct resources into the modernization of outdated industries, and the development of new manufacturing or industrial enterprises. The fishing industry in Guangdong province has undergone dramatic change. In 1990, there were only two deep-sea fishing boats in the port of Zhanjiang. By 1996, the number had risen to 141. From 1994 to 1995, total ocean catch for Guangdong province grew 13% to 1.5 million tons. Fish farms are also a growing industry in the region and include freshwater shrimp, eel, crab and abalone.

Other industries are also flourishing in rural areas. In the late 1970s, Huizhou city in Guangdong province, was a small village with no industrial production. Today, the city produces 60% of the country's telephone sets. It is also well-known for large screen televisions and mid-range hi-fi equipment.

Figure 2.10   China's fishery and seafood production

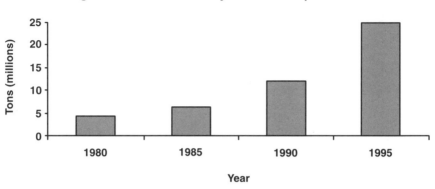

Data compiled from: Agricultural Development Report of China, 1996

In 1981, the TCL Group started a joint venture with initial liquid capital or cash of only RMB 5,000. By 1995, the TCL Group had sales of RMB 4.8 billion. Today, TCL's televisions are among the top three television brands in terms of market share in China.

Further industrialization in rural areas and the modernization of agriculture have a major role in the Ninth Five Year Plan (1996–2000). The government is committed to building 50 large agriculture-based enterprises with cutting edge technology and management techniques. The Ninth Five Year Plan also calls for the establishment of an additional 100 new rural high-tech Development Zones, and 300 Development Zones to support and enhance key local industries. By 2000, agriculture-related industries are expected to generate RMB 500 billion (US$60 billion), of which RMB 10 billion (US$1.2 billion) will be exported.

Finally, there is another significant group of consumers whose origins are rural, however, few statistics are available. These are the 100 million migrant workers in China. They come from the poorer rural areas and are on the move in search of work. In the cities, they do work that others do not want, often in construction, restaurants, retail and sanitation. The jobs they do pay well, often higher than average wages, and their incomes often equal that of salaried urban workers. They are adaptable, disciplined and anxious to do well. Their numbers and mobility might make accurate study impossible. This is, however, an urban consumer to be reckoned with; urban but still largely classified by the old Hukou system as "rural".

Generally, the qualitative nature of life is improving faster for rural residents than for any other consumer segment. Their work is being made easier and more profitable through modernization, leaving them more time for leisure, and money for consumption. Over the next 15 years, changes and improvements to daily life will transform many of them into urban residents.

The 60+ consumer

By 1996, the number of people over 60 years of age in China reached 110 million. No other country in the world has so many citizens over 60. In 1996, the over 60 sector numbered 110 million and represented 9% of China's total population. By 2000, the over 60 sector will grow to 130 million and represent 10% of China's total population. By 2050, their number is expected to climb to 370 million, or one-quarter of the total population.

The government has begun to recognize the growing importance of this sector by proclaiming September 9 "Senior's Day". On September 9, everyone is expected to do a good deed for the elderly. More significantly, a law has been issued protecting the rights and interests of all senior citizens. This does not signal a breakdown in the traditional respect for the aged, but underlines the harsh practicalities of the market system. With more and more people working

Figure 2.11 The growth of the 60+ population in China

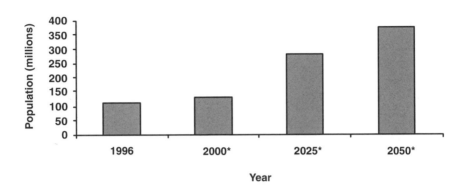

*Estimated figure
Data compiled from: Trends and Characteristics of Chinese Elderly, Chinese Academy of Social Science, 1995

longer hours there simply isn't anyone at home to care for the elderly. Today, China's average life expectancy is 69. Healthier living and improved medical care will inevitably push that number higher.

Traditionally, children took care of aging parents, but the market economy and the one-child per family policy make such traditions difficult to hold on to. Certainly, the market economy has brought higher incomes and more consumer goods to buy. It has also made workdays longer and time and energy scarcer. The one-child policy is terrific for the child, as they usually have two parents and four grandparents to spoil them. It is not so good for the parents and grandparents as one child can't practically be expected to support and care for six aging adults.

"Sending the elderly to seniors homes does not mean that the younger generation is shirking its responsibility. They just have no choice," said Mr. Baozhen Qiao, director of the Dongzhimen Senior

Home in Beijing. "They are too busy with their work. How can they spare time and energy to take care of a blind person? That is too much for them," added Ms. Deqing Yu, an 87-year-old resident of the home whose sight is severely impaired.

Many societies in the West have already shifted care for the elderly out of the home, and for much the same reasons. In the West we've also seen the boom in nursing homes and elderly care, but it will be nothing like the boom China will see. In Shanghai, there were 42 homes for seniors in 1978. By 1992, the number had grown to 500. Currently, Beijing has 300 and most are equipped with private rooms, reception areas, cafeterias, exercise rooms, medical staff and 24 hour service. Most of these homes are within reach of the average salaried households. At the Dongzhimen Senior Home in Beijing, monthly rates run from RMB 750 (US$96) to RMB 1,200 (US$154). The range in price depends on the amount of care the resident needs. Many retirees, especially those without spouses, are choosing to move into these facilities before their health might require such care. "Actually, I have less work here than I did at home, and there are many people to talk to," explained Ms. Fanxiu Zhou, also living at the Dongzhimen home. Added Mr. Wong, "Fewer topics of interest are shared between children and older people nowadays. I was kept out of their world...But there is no gap between us here. We live like a family."

Attitudes in China seem to change faster than products and services can be provided. Presently, there are only 730,000 senior citizens living in senior residences in China. But senior citizen homes are not the only thing in demand. In Shanghai, over 1,200 "Conversation Stations" have been built by neighborhoods as centers where the elderly can gather. And in Tianjin, "home help" is a growing service for the elderly. Specially trained attendants visit the elderly to clean, shop, cook or do odd jobs.

Due to the shortage of residences specifically for the elderly, and the increasing availability of housing generally, more and more seniors are living alone. By 1988, a survey of nine major cities in China showed that already 32.4% of the elderly lived alone, or away from their children. In the past, the decline of the size of the average Chinese family could be attributed to some of the children of multi-children families moving away to start families of their own. Today, the young go where the jobs and business opportunities are, often leaving parents alone and without the traditional care and support of their offspring.

Figure 2.12   The average size of Chinese families

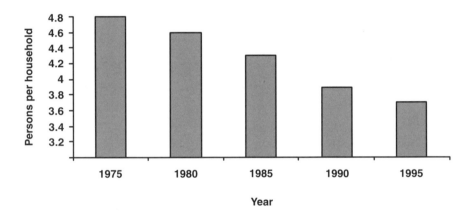

Data complied from: Chinese Academy of Social Science, 1996

Education has a direct correlation to consumer tastes and behavior. The population that will turn 60 in the next few years will have the highest overall jump in level of education of this group in the history of China. Of those currently 60+, only 30% have had some kind of organized formal education such as primary school. Of those turning 60 between now and the end of the century, 60% will have had some form of formal education.

Figure 2.13 Percentage of people with at least primary school education in China, 1994

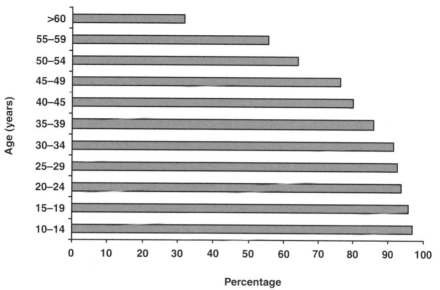

Data compiled from: China Population Statistics, 1995

Figure 2.14 Educational level of 60+ people in China

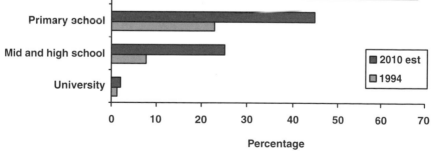

Data compiled from: China Population Statistics Yearbook, analysis of Deloitte Consulting, 1997

The generation that is only now turning 60 will have characteristics very different from its older counterparts. The difference is similar in scope to the distinction between children born into families before 1978, and the s-generation born after 1978.

The generation that is now turning 60 has watched the transformation of the past 20 years and has generally benefited from it. They are more sophisticated and will expect more from life in retirement than earlier generations of seniors. A 1988 survey of seniors showed that their level of consumption of "luxury" goods was only one-third that of their children. This has little to do with income as their household incomes were 60% higher than their children. The emerging group of seniors, those turning 60 between now and the turn of the century, are likely to have a greater appetite for luxury goods only because they have lived with them longer and have come to expect them as part of their standard of living.

Figure 2.15   Ownership of luxury items of young families and their 60+ parents' families, Changchuen, 1988

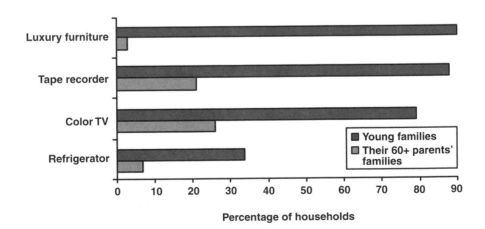

Data compiled from: Women's Association of the City of Changchuen, 1988

A recent survey in Beijing showed that the higher the level of education, the better the general health. No matter what the level of health, seniors 60 years and over are likely to spend three times as much on health care and health care products as those between the ages of 17 and 60.

A 1992 survey in Jiangsu province of 2,000 urban and rural seniors indicated that they spent only 0.6–0.7% of their total expenditures on entertainment. The higher the education, the greater the amount spent on intangibles such as entertainment, travel and education.

It is difficult to find accurate statistics on all aspects of life for the 110 million people in China now over 60. It is difficult to say how many live in poverty, or how much money they hold as a group. Generally, in rural areas, 64% are supported by their children, and 29% manage to live on the work they are still able to do and available social assistance. Of the urban elderly, 49% are able to get by on their own pensions, 14% survive on the work they can do, and the rest depend upon the support of their families.

There is a significant difference in personality between those now turning 60 and older seniors. Those turning 60 paid for China's prosperity and are anxious to enjoy it. They are more open-minded and have higher expectations than older citizens, and are more willing to travel and enjoy the time they now have for family and friends.

What is not changing for either urban or rural elderly is their desire to remain in close contact with their families. This may mean construction of senior's residences on expensive urban lands, or it may lead to urban planning that shifts urban workers and their extended families to better, more affordable housing in municipalities and suburbs on the outskirts of major cities. As time goes on, the nature of life for the elderly in China begins to resemble lifestyles in the West.

What misconceptions, metaphors, or personality traits best describe the three consumer segments discussed in this chapter? The s-generation is the first generation of the single-child family, but it is a fatal misconception for business strategists to see this enormous consumer segment as being made up of children. The s-generation is now gradually turning 18, leaving home, finding jobs and becoming adults. They will soon define and direct the most active consumer segment of any modern society, adults aged 18–35.

The West sees China as a nation dominated by an agricultural population. Young and middle-aged rural residents slaving behind oxen in muddy fields. Many of them traded the ox for a tractor long ago, and fields for shares in foreign invested enterprises. They are quickly becoming urban, so quickly that business strategists can only anticipate their location and impact, and must plan their strategies like hunters aiming well ahead of fast moving game.

The generation now turning 60 paid the price for China's new prosperity. They were born during war, grew up through civil strife, and survived the Cultural Revolution and China's long isolation. They want their piece of the pie, they want it now, and they want it before they're too old to enjoy it.

Endnote

[1] In China, almost every city has a certain percentage of land designated as rural areas, hence the population from these areas is labeled as rural residents.

Chapter 3

Pioneering

New consumer centers

The overall purpose of this book is to explore and explain as best as possible China's consumer boom. One of the characteristics of this boom is its ever changing nature. It is changing fast and from so many different forces and directions that fixing specific definitions is difficult. Because of its ever-changing nature, this text has focused on the fundamental underlying social, cultural and economic influences to explain the means and motivations of consumers, directing attention at the newest, most active developments, developments that will have a significant long-term impact.

In the previous chapter, we looked at emerging consumer groups. In this chapter we will explore innovations in economic development that have created three new emerging consumer centers: satellite cities, coastal cities and resource-rich regions. Interestingly, these three emerging consumer centers have been shaped as much by ideas, as by practical need or circumstance.

We all understand why a sheltered harbor would lead to a portside community that would attract commerce. But China's economy is moving so fast that State planners, and others, are planning and developing communities long before there is any infrastructure to support it. The best example of this large-scale planning is the Suzhou special industrial park launched in 1994 with assistance and support from Singapore.

The idea for the China–Singapore Suzhou Industrial Park came from the former prime minister of Singapore, Lee Kuan Yew. Suzhou was already an important city in China with an ancient history and a population of 1.4 million, located 85 km west of Shanghai up the Yangzi River. It is perhaps because of its location in the thriving Yangzi Delta Region that it was chosen as the site for this ambitious experiment. The concept was borrowed from a similarly planned community in Singapore called Jurong Town and is designed to integrate industrial sites, residential areas and commercial space. The Suzhou development will eventually occupy 70 km², and engage a highly-skilled workforce of 350,000. On-site housing will accommodate 600,000. A few years ago the site was open farmland. Today, it is home to foreign companies such as Black & Decker, Advanced Micro Devices, Eli Lilly, Samsung, Siemens and Becton Dickson, among others.

Singapore has brought capital as well as ideas to Suzhou and many of the factories in Suzhou have close ties with related operations in Singapore. Singapore has been given considerable free reign to develop the industrial park in part because China is hoping to learn more from Singapore than how to make money. Chinese leaders admire Singapore's clean, safe and relatively crime-free streets, all of which are growing concerns for China.

The industrial park, essentially a city within a city, is governed by a group of Chinese officials chaired by the mayor of Suzhou. They set policy for the park and are responsible for approving investments. They spend a considerable amount of time in Singapore studying other aspects of Singapore's social and economic system including public housing development, environmental control, security, factory safety and customs management. One of the earliest programs they brought to Suzhou from Singapore was a fund that offers retirement savings and social security benefits to employees. Employees can even draw on the fund for housing and medical expenses.

For China, this kind of "satellite" allows controlled economic development. It is also a transportable concept and will play a large part in the development of the resource-rich regions of the interior — clearly, an idea whose time has come. But it is a very different process than the traditional development or re-development of existing commercial centers upon existing infrastructures. Suzhou Industrial Park is ambitious, but it seems to be working well, as it has already attracted a total of 234 projects with an overall investment of US$2.3 billion. Of these 234 projects, 179 are funded by international investors. In fact, the rapid development of industrial parks in Suzhou has pushed the city up to the nation's 4th largest city in terms of GPP, although its urban population ranks only the 45th in the country.

These new economic centers are creating dynamic new consumer markets. They are also drawing existing consumers from established economic centers. Focusing on these new centers addresses Western misconceptions about the size, importance and location of consumer markets. Business strategists targeting only cities of one million or more fail to address the significant numbers of sophisticated consumers in newer coastal cities. Focusing on the core population of larger cities omits the consumers in satellites on the outskirts. Believing that inland regions are filled with rural people living in the Stone Age completely neglects astonishing but inevitable developments in the resource-rich regions of the west.

Satellite cities

"Satellite cities" is the term used to describe the migration of people from traditional city centers to suburbs, economic zones, or industrial parks. Traditionally, people were drawn to the city for the services and opportunities it offered. Now, for a number of reasons, the migration is reversed

The most practical reasons for people to move from the city centers to the suburbs are the abundant and affordable housing they offer and the growing job opportunities. China's city centers were not designed to accommodate excessive residential housing. Limited availability of land for development and high cost make downtown

Figure 3.1   Urban population flow model

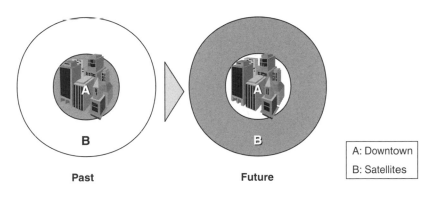

Past   Future

A: Downtown
B: Satellites

residential construction impractical. Whatever traditional housing that remains is quickly being taken over for commercial construction of hotels and office buildings. But the market for residential construction is driven by more than high cost and limited supply. Chinese leaders assumed that the economy would rest on the automotive industry, much as it does in the United States. They believed that China's newly affluent citizens would put cars at the top of their shopping list; but the population's needs were far more fundamental. After years of turmoil and instability people yearned for shelter they could call their own. As a result, the government has decided to redirect attention from the automotive industry to the development of the residential construction industry, as it is the driving engine of China's economy today. Following the Ninth Five Year Plan (1996–2000), Beijing allocated 20 km^2 for housing. The intention is to raise the per capita living space of residents from 8.7 m^2 (1995) to 16.5 m^2 by the year 2000. This involves residential construction of seven million m^2 per year for the next 15 years. Significantly, the vast majority of this residential construction will not occur in existing city centers.

Migration away from city centers does not mean a decrease in urban population. The total urban population in China is growing.

This is a result of the growth of satellite communities, modern, high-tech, efficient communities that are attached to, or plugged into, existing urban centers or transportation infrastructures. Essentially, the new satellite cities are urban areas. The actual size of China's urban areas is expanding in relation to the proliferation of satellite cities. Where the trend differs from Western suburbanization of the 1940s and 1950s is in its rapid growth. From 1990 to 2010, China's urban population is expected to grow from 27% to 50% of the total population, or an additional 400 million urban citizens. It took Europe 2000 years to achieve such a profound level of urbanization on such a large scale. In China, it will occur in only two decades.

One of the most significant economic developments of the past 17 years is the establishment of the Pudong New Area just east of Shanghai. The Pudong New Area is a special economic zone

Figure 3.2   China's official urban population

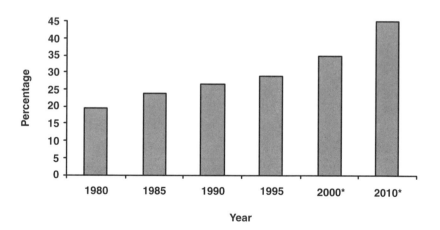

*Estimated population
Data compiled from: China Statistical Yearbook, Analysis and Forecast of Social Development of China 1995–1996, Chinese Industry and Commerce Press, 1996

composed of four development zones including a finance and trade zone, a tax-free zone, a free-trade zone and an export processing zone. The combination of close proximity to Shanghai and the freer economic environment of a special economic zone have allowed the Pudong New Area to support and accelerate Shanghai's race to become a major international financial center.

The area has been particularly attractive to foreign investors with 35% of the Pudong's GDP coming from internationally funded firms. In 1995, an additional 640 foreign-invested projects began operations in the Pudong New Area with a total investment of US$2.8 billion. Also in 1995, exports from the Pudong reached US$2.3 billion, an increase of 21% over the previous year. The area recorded a GDP of US$4.1 billion from January to September of 1995, a 17.2% increase from the year before. Total tax revenue from the Pudong in 1995 reached US$493 million.

Hong Kong has acted as China's window on the world for many years. Until the late 1980s, almost all of China's imports, exports and foreign exchange were processed through Hong Kong. As Shanghai developed it began to assume more and more of Hong Kong's roles. Since the appearance of development zones like the Pudong New Area, and the expansion and modernization of other existing ports, international trade to and from China through Hong Kong has declined to 40% of China's total international trade. Hong Kong will certainly continue to prosper, perhaps stronger than ever, but its relative economic position to cities and regions in China will decline.

The Pudong has ambitions to challenge Hong Kong's role as China's banker in the future. In 1996, the central government opened RMB transactions to international banks in the Pudong New Area. As of March 1997, a total of eight international banks with branches in the Pudong had been given authorization to deal in RMB including Citibank, Hong Kong and Shanghai Banking Corporation, and the Industrial Bank of Japan, clear moves by the central government to return Shanghai to its former status as a regional financial center and the "Paris of the East".

The new economic centers that are most like real "satellites" follow the example set by Singapore's industrial park in Suzhou. Economically, the park has been a tremendous success and continues to attract significant foreign investment. Netherlands-based Phillips Electronics invested US$96 million in the Suzhou Television Factory in 1992, and followed with a US$24.5 million investment in a joint venture with Suzhou Chunhua Vacuum Cleaner Factory. American pharmaceutical giant Upjohn has two projects going, a US$30 million joint venture and a new US$15 million project. Taiwan funded Acer Peripherals Suzhou Co. Ltd. recently upped its investment from US$12 million to US$18 million.

Chongqing, in Sichuan province, is the largest city in the world with a population exceeding 30 million. The growth of Chongqing is the result of a number of factors including an amalgamation of existing communities, the ongoing resettlement of up to one million people displaced by the Three Gorges Dam project, and the general economic boom. Chongqing has played a major role in the modern history of China, and is set to become one of China's key economic city states behind Beijing, Shanghai and Tianjin.

Chiang Kai Shek chose Chongqing as his wartime capital in part because of its isolation and a severity of climate that made attack by air impractical. After 1949, Chongqing's strategic importance continued, as its isolation inland offered continuing security for the development of China's military industries, and heavy industries such as steel, machinery, electronics, chemicals and textiles. Today, Chongqing is also the home of China's biggest motorcycle manufacturer, China Jialing Industrial Company. There are over 300 motorcycle component parts manufacturers in the city employing 300,000 workers.

Much of the growth of the population of Chongqing in recent years is as a result of the gradual industrialization and urbanization of small towns and villages surrounding the old city center. The new municipal boundary of the city encloses a largely urban population. This process of industrialization and urbanization is perhaps more organic and "natural" than the careful planning and administration of other satellite cities like Suzhou and the Pudong but it is, nevertheless, a form of satellite growth.

In 1991, Beijing established the Beijing Economic and Technological Development Area (BDA). It is located 17 km from Beijing in the Yizhuang area. The BDA plans to develop 15 km^2 in the first phase of its development. Infrastructure construction on a core 4.3 km^2 has already been completed. A telecommunications center has been installed that offers 100,000 ends of digital phone lines supported by fiber optic cables. One senior official commented, "Our target for the BDA is to create a city within a city. The zone will become a new modern city with a population of 400,000 to 500,000. It will be an export-oriented production base with an industrial output value of RMB 30 billion by the year 2000." Many international blue chip companies have already established operations in the zone including Bayer, Rhone-Poulenc, AT&T, GE, SMC, ABB, Kimberley-Clark and Unilever. Local companies have also shifted operations there including Beijing Changxin, International Sport Recreation Co. Ltd. and Beijing Zhongcai Painting Co. Ltd. Baoxiang International Garment Centre plans to invest more than RMB 1 billion in a huge 66 hectare production center.

Between 1991 and 1994, Beijing expropriated 33 km^2 annually for development. Presently, there are 30 Development Zones and industrial parks spread over a total of 42 km^2. By 2010, up to one-half of Beijing's residents will live in the satellite communities surrounding Beijing. These satellite communities include Huilongguan, Beiyuan, Wangjing, Dongba, Dingfuzhuang, Nanyuan and Fengtai.

In 1996, Beijing's population reached 12.5 million. According to State planners, the population should not have reached 12.5 million until 2010. Much of this influx is blamed on the arrival or resettlement of migrant workers.

Today, there are only four underground mass transit railways in China, one each in Beijing, Tianjin, Shanghai and Guangzhou. The development of satellite communities has led to an increased demand for the development of mass transit railways. Of the 30 largest cities in China, all with populations exceeding one million, 21 are developing a total of 33 lines of subways and rail transit systems with a total length of 649 km.

Shanghai's subway system has been instrumental in furthering development in the south west of the city. The subway is being extended south another 5.76 km. The town of Xinzhuang is located along the new extension of the subway line. A residential development came on the market soon after the subway line opened. The first lot of 58 apartments sold out in two days.

Commercial activities in Chinese cities are being transformed by the movement of residents from the traditional city centers to satellite communities. Markets follow consumers and traditional city centers are losing their role as the only distribution centers for goods and services. Nanjing Road East in Shanghai is one of the most famous shopping streets in all of China. A recent survey, however, showed that pedestrian traffic has declined in the past few years from two million per day to 800,000. Many major downtown department and specialty stores across China, from Shanghai to Urumqi, are seeing a stagnation or decline in their retail sales figures. This is after a decade of double digit growth. Increased competition in downtown centers plays a role here, but one of the most important factors is the movement of consumers to outlying satellite communities. Of course this phenomenon presents huge opportunities to astute business strategists. Recently, the Japanese warehouse retailer Yaohan

Corporation opened one of its superstores in Huwenlu at the south west end of Shanghai's existing subway line. Mr. Yasunaga, Director and General Manager of Yaohan Shanghai Holdings Ltd, says growing suburban populations will bring more shopping dollars to the firms' investments. Domestic enterprises are following this trend with Nonggongshang Supermarkets, one of Shanghai's biggest chains, recently opening two 4,000 m² supermarkets in Jinyang in the Pudong area. The chain plans to open an additional ten outlets in the Pudong in 1997.

Satellite cities are not merely attracting more and more residents and commerce. In fact, they are changing the landscape of city centers and suburbs in China. In many cases, the satellite cities are developing so fast and economically strong that they are leaving the original city centers to become their commercial and residential suburbs.

Obviously, the consumer migration presents opportunities and challenges to existing distribution networks. It also creates a challenge to marketers. Should marketing campaigns be directed at urban residents of traditional city centers, or urban residents of satellite communities? What is the real difference in their needs and tastes? When international car manufacturers entered the China market in the 1980s, almost all of them directed their marketing campaigns at urban institutional buyers and residents in traditional city centers. Which group is now the most representative? Which group has the most disposable income? China is a changing landscape of challenging issues.

New coastal cities

The central government expects the greatest economic activity and population density to settle into five city zones. The first is the Pearl

River Delta Region. This was one of the first areas to benefit from economic reforms and international investment. The second zone is the Yangzi River Delta which has had its economic development fueled by the Pudong special economic zone. The third zone is the Beijing-Tianjin-Tangshan Delta. This zone has attracted a great deal of international investment because of Beijing's role as capital and seat of government. The final two regions are the Jiaodong Peninsula and the Liaodong Peninsula. Because of their geographic location, these zones are particularly attractive to Japanese, Korean and European investors. They also benefit from an excellent transportation infrastructure and readily available skilled labor.

A thriving coastal region with over 3,300 km of mainland coastline has taken shape in Fujian province. The area includes five major cities, Fuzhou, Putian, Quanzhou, Xiamen and Zhangzhou. The total population of the region is 19 million, of which 35% is urban. The region has benefited from special economic zones, coastal cities, economic and technological development zones, Taiwanese-invested zones and bonded zones. Interestingly, considering their adversarial histories, by the end of August 1995, a total of US$4 billion had been invested in the region from Taiwan.

Before the economic reforms of 1978, the percentage of the population in the region that could be classified urban fell below the national average. The region's rapid urbanization was fueled in part by the same economic reforms that created the boom regions of the Pearl River and Yangzi River Deltas. The attributes that make the coastal region different from the river delta regions are the investment and influence crossing from Taiwan, and investment from the many overseas Chinese who see the region as their ancestral home. By 1995, the GNP of the region reached RMB 158.2 billion (US$19 billion), or 70% of Fujian's total GNP.

From 1980 to 1994, China's total urban population increased by 120 million. Of this new urban population, 50% live in the coastal region. Since 1982, in Guangdong province, the total area occupied by urban residents jumped 100% to 1,676 km². There are other successful coastal cities besides Shenzen and Zhuhai including Shuende, Dongwu, Zhongshan, Fanyu, Fushan and Nanhai, all of which were established after 1978.

Figure 3.3   China's cities

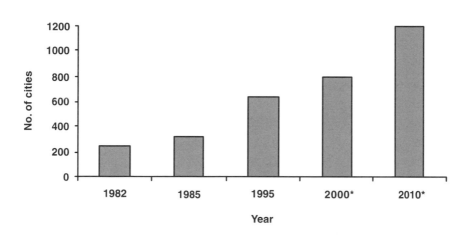

*Estimated growth
Data compiled from: China Statistical Yearbook, Chinese Industry and Commerce Press, 1996

In 1995, of China's 640 officially classified cities, 270 are in the coastal region. Many of these cities have existed for centuries as settlement has always been drawn to the plentiful deep-water ports along China's east coast. As the economy draws more rural residents from farming to centers of commerce, the numbers and sizes of China's cities and towns have mushroomed.

Officially, a town is a community that, generally, has a county level government, or has at least 2,000 urban residents with a total

Figure 3.4   China's towns

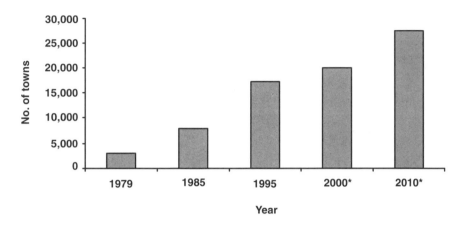

*Estimated growth
Data compiled from: China Statistical Yearbook, China's Ninth Five Year Plan for Economic and Social Development and Its Targets for 2010, Chinese Industry and Commerce Press, 1996

population of about 20,000. By 1995 in China, 1,500 towns had been established through a combination of the expansion of farmers' collectives, the joint investment of farmers, and the additional population attracted to this commerce. The majority of these towns sprang up in the Pearl River and Yangzi River Deltas.

The central government has been hard-pressed to keep pace with the rapid urbanization of China's booming economic regions. The Ninth Five Year Plan has focused attention on the development of the Bohai Bay region and the Yellow River Delta. In the Bohai Bay region alone, RMB 1 trillion (US$120 billion) has been allocated for infrastructure development from now until 2010.

The rapid urbanization and industrialization of the Pearl River Delta was triggered in the late 1970s by the establishment of the special economic zone of Shenzhen. A similar boom in the Yangzi River Delta followed the establishment of the Pudong region of Shanghai.

Figure 3.5   China's official urban population

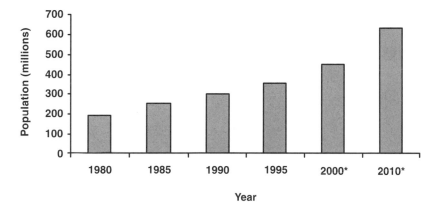

*Estimated growth
Data compiled from: China Statistical Yearbook, Chinese Industry and Commerce Press, 1996

By 1995, the total number of towns in China reached 15,000; by 2010, this number will almost double to 27,000. By 1995, the total number of cities had reached 640. The total number of cities in China is expected to double by 2010 to 1,200. In 1995, the total urban population was 350 million, by 2010 that number should grow to 700 million.

The primary interest in discussing the development of the coastal region is its rapid urbanization, or the dramatic increase of the percentage of the population officially classified as urban. These are consumers with high disposable income, and rapidly expanding material expectations. However, that is a very broad definition and seems to suggest that rural residents may not be consumers worthy of marketers' attention. That would be a mistake, as individual rural residents are often wealthier than comparably skilled urban residents. The traditional definitions of each group were established more than 50 years ago and relied more on geography than skills, tastes, or expectations.

If a family was defined as rural, the definition would stick and would be passed down from generation to generation no matter how circumstances might have changed. Often "rural" residents of the coastal region, especially rural residents in areas close to major cities, are much wealthier than their urban counterparts because they possess land. Possession, or right of usage, is a more accurate description in China than ownership, but right of usage can be exchanged or sold for equity just as easily as ownership. The urbanization of rural residents often begins when they give up their land to domestic or international companies for development. They receive cash or shares in the purchasing company. If the government expropriates the land they receive cash or some other form of reimbursement. Often, the capital from such a sale would be invested in a small family business such as a restaurant, a shop, or a small manufacturing enterprise. Though many of these industrialized entrepreneurs are still officially classified as rural, their tastes and means and behavior as consumers is urban.

The current urbanization of China is following two routes. The first occurs when areas adjacent to larger cities are expropriated for residential or industrial development. The second process of urbanization is through industrialization. The best examples of this process is in the Pearl River and Yangzi River Deltas, but industrialization has occurred in other coastal regions as well. From 1990 to 1995, Fujian province lost a total of 33,200 hectares of cultivated land to industrial and residential development. The population in the province grew 1.64 million between 1990 and 1995, and per capita cultivated land dropped from 0.0413 to 0.038 hectares. In 1994, in Guangdong province a total of 1.76 million acres of farmland was lost to residential or industrial development. In 1978, there was only one city in all of Guangdong province with a population in excess of 500,000; today there are four.

From 1991 to 1994, Beijing expropriated a total of 130 km^2 for development. The annual rate of expropriation was approximately 33 km². Of this, 10 km² was land that fell within the definition of urban land and 23 km² was taken from outlying rural lands. Of the total 130 km², 44 km² went into industrial development, 24 km² into residential development and the rest was taken by infrastructure development. Of the 24 km² of housing development, less than 10 km² came from urban lands, the remainder was appropriated from outlying lands. Expropriation is reaching further and further into the countryside and is now closing in on the outlying communities of Huilongguan, Lishuiqiao, Baiyuan and Wangjing.

A typical example of the increasing urbanization and industrial development of smaller communities is the boom town of Beijiao in the heart of the Pearl River Delta. Ten years ago, Beijiao was a small farming community producing rice and sugar cane. Industrialization began in earnest in 1986. Presently, Beijiao is the country's top manufacturer of microwave ovens and the world's largest manufacturer of electric fans. Industrialization has also spread to the agriculture of the region and Beijiao now boasts the biggest eel and chicken processing and exporting center in the country. Manufactured goods are exported to over 50 countries worldwide. Annual export value now exceeds US$200 million.

Industrialization and wealth has brought infrastructure improvements including public transport and a modern telecommunication system. In March 1996, Beijiao was chosen as the site for a scientific research and development center involving a total investment of US$144 million. A high-technology college is being constructed to train managers, economists and engineers for positions in developing regions of the central and western Pearl River Delta.

The development of the coastal region and the increasing urbanization it entails creates yet another new and evolving market for consumer goods and services. The coastal cities that dominated the first years of the economic reforms, Beijing, Shanghai and

Guangzhou, are no longer isolated phenomena or even typical of coastal regions generally. The consumer market is becoming diffuse and pervasive and has become an even greater challenge to marketers, entrepreneurs and investors than the complex, frantic and fast changing environment of China's urban centers of the 1980s.

Resource-rich regions

The economic development of the past 17 years has had its greatest impact along the coastal regions of the country. The first wave of this economic growth has been labor and technology based. China's Ninth Five Year Plan aims at sustaining this economic growth and ensuring that development spreads throughout the country. The second wave of economic growth will be resource based and infrastructure driven. Growth will also be directed inland to poor but resource-rich regions.

The economic gap between coastal regions and the middle and western regions of China is dramatic. To compensate for this imbalance, the central government will focus its efforts on improving the infrastructure construction necessary for making these resource-rich regions economically viable for foreign and domestic industries and investors. The government is also encouraging the transfer of some industries from the eastern and coastal areas inland, particularly those industries that are labor intensive, or consume high levels of energy or resources. In addition, the government has expanded the power of local governments in these resource-rich but isolated regions, to approve internationally-invested enterprises. Local governments now have the authority to approve internationally-invested projects of up to US$30 million. These innovations, or advantages, have had no detrimental economic impact on the thriving coastal regions. Generally, the central government is moving away from policies to control or administer economic development to a more hands off and market-oriented approach.

The greatest hindrance to the development of China's vast store of natural resources has been the lack of sufficient transportation infrastructure. Recently, to accelerate growth inland, the Ninth Five Year Plan has allocated funding for the extension of the national railway system into the north west and south west regions. A total of 5,295 km of railway will be added with a transportation capacity of 325 million tons. Five regional railways will also be added with a total of 2,651 km of railway and a transportation capacity of 70 million tons.

Not all regions are waiting for central government initiatives. The province of Guizhou, a mountainous province in the south west of China, began a 121 km railway between Liupanshui and Buoguo in the western part of the province. The estimated cost of construction is RMB 2.8 billion and it is the first railway system initiated and financed by local government. The railway will connect the mineral-rich region of the province to the national south west railway network.

Exploration of the interior and western provinces serves a more fundamental purpose than the development of isolated regions. Industrial development throughout China consumes greater and greater amounts of electricity, electricity that is generated with water, coal or oil; and there are still 100 million people in China without electricity. Currently, China's per capita annual electricity usage is only 650 watts compared with 11,000 watts in the US.

The resource-rich regions have abundant reserves of much needed coal, oil and natural gas. Developing these resources is essential to sustain the rapid economic development of the country. Effective development of these inland regions is also critical to reducing the economic disparities between these regions and coastal regions. This balancing of regional development will reinforce social stability and contribute to sustained, healthy, long-term economic development.

China's demand for electrical energy has increased 5% annually since the beginning of the economic reforms. The International Energy Agency predicts this demand will continue to grow at 4.2% annually until 2010. In 1995, China's electrical generating capacity was 214 GW, by 2000, capacity should reach 300 GW. To meet these energy levels China will depend on thermal generating power plants

Figure 3.6   China's electricity generating capacity

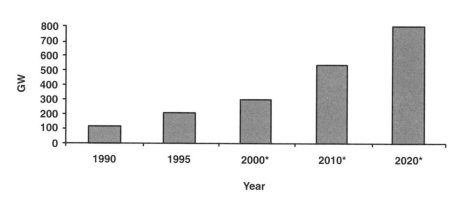

*Estimated figures
Data compiled from: China's Ministry of Electric Power, China National Electric Power Design Institute, 1996

in the coal-rich regions of Inner Mongolia, Ningxia, Shaanxi, Shanxi, Yunnan, Guizhou and Henan. The Ninth Five Year Plan calls for the development of 19 large-scale hydropower stations to be built in the country. The combined total output of these new sources will be 27 GW by 2000, one-tenth of current overall production.

The extent and economic potential of China's natural resources is staggering. China has sufficient known coal, oil and natural gas reserves to supply its own needs for many decades to come. Presently, China produces 1.3 billion tons of coal annually. Of this production,

30 million tons is exported. Recently, The Ministry of the Coal Industry announced agreements totaling US$5.3 billion in foreign investment in China's coal industry. This investment will go toward greater modernization of the industry and result in increased and more efficient production.

China's largest developed oil field is located in Daqing, in the north east province of Heilongjiang. Daqing will produce 50 million tons annually until at least 2005, but these reserves are now in decline. Since the late 1980s, the government has focused on stabilizing production in the east and increasing exploration in the west. Exploration in the west has revealed tremendous, and as yet, untapped reserves. In 1995, production of crude oil from the Xinjiang Uygur Autonomous Region was 12.8 million tons. It is estimated that the region contains up to three billion tons of crude oil with 1.9 billion tons of reserves already verified. Total production should increase to 26 million tons by 2000, and 50 million tons by 2010. In 1995, China National Petroleum Corporation (CNPC) produced a total of 140 million tons of crude oil. By 2000, CNPC hopes to see total production rise to 145–150 million tons annually.

By 1995, total natural gas production was 16 billion m^3. By 2000, further discoveries from fields inland and from offshore drilling, should increase total production to 20–25 billion m^3.

Foreign companies have begun serious exploration and development in the Tarin Basin including Exxon and the Italian firm Agip. After the discovery of the huge reserves in the Tarin Basin in 1978, China began construction of a 522 km highway through the 560,000 km^2 desert basin. This highway has opened up the region for investment and settlement and has led to the construction of a major petrochemical complex and two fertilizer plants. Presently, oil is transported from the region by truck. Construction of a major pipeline should begin by 2000.

As the coastal regions flourished, State planners recognized the need to shift attention and investment to the development of the interior and western provinces. The development process begins with the discovery of the natural resource. Highways are constructed to bring in labor and materials and export the resource to existing refineries or processing plants elsewhere. Finally, refineries and processing plants are built close to the source of the discovery and secondary industries spring up to support a growing population of consumers.

Chapter 4

New Times, New Realities

Life in transition

So far, the concrete changes that have led to China's consumer boom have been outlined and discussed. The concrete changes are those that are solidly tangible and most importantly, measurable and verifiable. We know when the reforms began and can trace their effect on China's GDP. China's industrialization and the policy of shifting economic development inland has led to the development of the natural resources needed to fuel the continued industrialization across the country and to fuel economic development in the inland regions, which has led to the creation of a large number of new emerging consumer centers. These are fairly simple cause and effect phenomena.

The way people live in China is in rapid transition. Each individual lives slightly differently than any other individual. Nevertheless, significant trends can be identified. The trends that will have the greatest impact on consumer spending can be broken down into three categories: three-dimensional living; a nation on the move; and apartment-bound.

Three-dimensional living

Three-dimensional living may seem an odd way to describe lives that include social activities such as bowling, mahjong and opera. These activities are options for social interchange and enrichment we in the West are accustomed to having. We may, in fact, take them for granted. During the Cultural Revolution, these activities, and many others, were branded as capitalist and bourgeois and officially forbidden. People's lives unfolded in two areas, the home and immediate neighborhood, or the workunit. During this time, the government wanted people to eat at the work unit, sleep at the workunit, and devote all their energy to the party and the great socialist revolution. The term "three-dimensional living" has been chosen because these social activities are now re-entering or entering the lives of many Chinese, bringing a depth and richness to lives that had been so constrained as to be one- or two-dimensional and therefore flat and lifeless.

During the Cultural Revolution there were only eight operas and perhaps a dozen movies available for the general population. They were not made for entertainment or enrichment but for propaganda. If people went, they went because they had to, or because they had no other choices. In Beijing at the time, there were only a dozen restaurants that might be comfortable and decent enough to invite guests to. Generally, life was made up of work and home. However, times have changed, and all the options open to us in the West for socializing, entertainment or enrichment are available for those in China who want it and can afford to pay for it. There are restaurants at every street corner serving every imaginable kind of food from every corner of the country and the world. There are karaoke clubs, discos, bars, 24-lane bowling alleys and even gambling casinos. The most striking aspect of the reappearance of these social outlets is the speed of their arrival and acceptance into the mainstream. In the 1980s, discos, karaoke clubs or western style bars could only be found in five star hotels. Chinese citizens could only enter if they had considerable means and the appropriate connections. Today, less than a decade later, discos and karaoke bars can be found in the smallest towns and villages throughout China. The constraints of the Cultural Revolution have given way to a new world of pleasure and amusement and consumers are rushing to spend more and more of their earnings to explore all the available entertainment.

Generally, young salaried workers spend 3–4 nights of the week out on the town. Besides the large variety of nightspots available,

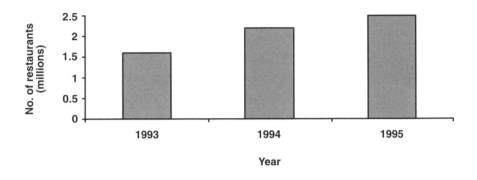

Figure 4.1   Growth of restaurants in China

Data compiled from: China Statistical Yearbook, various years

there are increasing numbers of 24-hour shops and restaurants and even movie theaters springing up to accommodate these night owls. Near to the National Gallery of Art in Beijing there is a restaurant called Meals for 24-hours. The restaurant was established in 1990 and was the first 24-hour restaurant in the capital. In June 1995, the first 24 hour grocery store, Tejibian, opened in Beijing. Three more stores are now planned. Since 1995, other 24-hour grocers have opened in Beijing including Beitaipingzhuang Food Supermarket and Zhongcong Food and Convenience Store. All find sales consist-ent and busy whether day or night.

By 1993, international businesses began to move into the 24-hour market with Baskin-Robbins Ice Cream and Cake Creation leading the way. But 24-hour shopping is not exclusive to Beijing, in fact it's more popular and was established earlier in Shanghai and Guangzhou. In this case though it is the idea, rather than any particular marketing innovation that has been taken up so quickly. I noticed 24-hour restaurants in the north western city of Urumqui. The difference was that they were offering lamb noodles and soup dumplings instead of the fried rice offered in Beijing. The phenomena is more profound than simply the notion of offering products and services around the clock. There is a greater desire to spend more time alone or with others away from home or work. Some of this can be classified as socializing or entertainment, but a significant portion of this time is also given over to education and advancement. As competition increases, the need for academic upgrading and skill enhancement becomes critical.

I spent some time looking into the kind and range of courses being offered and found that different courses appealed to different age groups. Children were interested in music lessons, especially piano and violin, painting, calligraphy, dancing and computer training. Adults preferred language training, computer training, typing, business administration, and general education courses at high school and university levels. Most of these courses are offered in the evening or on weekends. Courses appealing to seniors are more esoteric and include horticulture, calligraphy, literature, painting, Qigong and more general education courses at the college level. Certainly, one of the key areas of interest is in language training. Anyone interested in business or management needs to learn English. Many young people and middle-aged professionals want to work for foreign firms, where the working environment is more comfortable and salaries higher, but where a foreign language is necessary. English is the second language of choice in China and is recognized as the language to have for any business or professional career of international scope.

The personal computer is transforming lives in China as much as it is anywhere. The desire for computer training and the perception that success is unattainable without computer skills has led to a proliferation of night classes. Behind the Beijing Hotel in downtown Beijing is a primary school with the charming name of Sweet Water Well Primary School. Computer courses have been offered at night since 1994. Admission is open to anyone with the price of tuition, and the students' ages range from 20 to 60. Among the students on any given night, you might find doctors, police officers, translators, managers, professors, waiters and waitresses, or the unemployed. In December 1994, a journalist from the *Beijing Daily* stopped a student and asked her why she was taking the course. She told him that she was an administrator at the International Convention Centre and that it took her two hours to travel to and from the course. She said, "I don't plan to change my job. I won't have a chance to use a computer for awhile once this training course is complete. Nevertheless, I feel the future will be all about computers. You will be at a disadvantage if you don't know how to use computers." Another young woman who was a worker at a State factory added, "The newspapers are full of talk about restructuring and bankruptcy. The company I work for is losing money. One day it might go bankrupt. I might have to go out and find another job. I'm still young and might want to change jobs, but if you look at all the ads for jobs, they all require a foreign language and computer skills!"

Of the 16 students in the class that night, 13 were paying for the training out of their own pockets, and 11 of the 16 were preparing themselves for future employment and would not be using the skills they were learning at their present jobs. Only two of the 16 had personal computers at home, but 12 planned to buy one. Of these students, seven had recently attended other training courses such as foreign language courses, accounting and tourist management.

From February to December of 1994, a total of 800 adult students had attended classes in the two small computer rooms at Sweet Water Well Primary School. The curriculum focused on hardware applications, computer-assisted accounting, document management and Chinese and English typewriting.

Most job advertisements in English language newspapers in China today do not specify that applicants be either foreign or domestic.

In the early 1980s, when foreign companies began setting up operations in China, few local Chinese had the language or management skills necessary for anything but the most rudimentary clerical work. Foreign companies were forced to bring whatever skilled management they needed with them, at considerable expense. However, the employment field is changing and local Chinese are now often as qualified, or more qualified in both multi-language and management skills than foreign staff. This is a direct result of the growing emphasis on higher education, and the energy of an extremely competitive and lucrative job market for those with the skills in greatest demand.

In March 1997, more than 1,700 firms attended the Talent and Property Exchange Fair for Beijing Suburban Rural Enterprises in Beijing. The three-day fair provided an opportunity for managers of rural enterprises to hire 1,500 technicians and managers. The purpose of the fair, organized by the Beijing municipal government, was to help improve management and product quality in local rural enterprises. Rural enterprises are undergoing a strategic shift from a focus on "extensive growth", or capital construction or investment, to "intensive growth", or growth achieved through the upgrading of management or improved production practices. Many highly qualified local professionals now command a monthly salary in excess of US$4,000. This is an obvious incentive to attend courses to upgrade skills.

The retail industry in China has been experiencing an unprecedented boom. Shopping is a favorite pastime for many. Stores in China generally stay open until 8 pm seven days a week. Many people enjoy shopping in the evening because of the bustling nighttime atmosphere, and also as a way to relax after a long day at work. Some believe in the traditional concept that a walk in the evening will help you live to age 99.

Foreign retailers have been expanding aggressively into China,

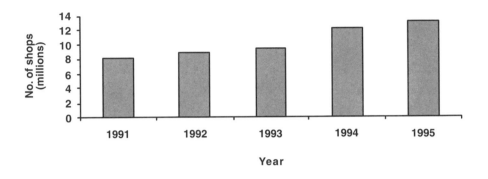

Figure 4.2   Growth of retail shops in China

Data compiled from: China Statistical Yearbook, various years

including such names as Wal-Mart of the US, Printemps of France, Yaohan of Japan and Makro of the Netherlands. With foreign retailers, come foreign brand-name products including such well-known fashion and cosmetic names as Prada, Pierre Cardin, Burburry, Bally, Liz Claiborne, Benetton and Yves St. Laurent.

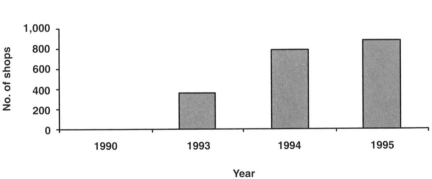

Figure 4.3   Growth of foreign retail shops in China

Data compiled from: China Statistical Yearbook, various years

The growth of the retail industry has led to the shopping mall. To keep customers happy, and attract new customers, developers began adding musical fountains, cafes and other amusements. More leisure time and increased disposable income has led to a boom in the development of theme parks designed to appeal to the whole family. More than 40 large theme parks have opened in the past decade, and most investors, both foreign and domestic, expect to get their money back in 3–5 years.

There are a number of theme parks near Shenzhen, in Guangdong province, including Splendid China and China Folk Culture Villages. Both parks reproduce China's history and culture in miniature. Window on the World, also near Shenzhen, is owned by a Chinese domestic company — China Travel Ltd. — and is more international in its outlook. Window on the World opened in 1994, the year the five-day work week became standard, and has seen 6,000–10,000 visitors a day. There are more than 100 famous landmarks from around the world, but the most amazing feature is its importation of foreign citizens as "attractions". Long-legged blondes and tattooed punks with spiked hair make themselves available for photographs with park guests.

A similar project is planned for Beijing. Asia-Pacific Family Centre will be divided into different sections representing different parts of the world. In the Japanese section, visitors will be able to eat sushi and watch Sumo wrestlers. They will also be able to watch a reproduction of the atomic blast at Hiroshima. In the American section, there will be stereotypical cops and robbers, and cowboys and Indians, and a chance to glimpse the daily life of the President of the United States.

Today, these parks are appealing to a generation just beginning to explore and appreciate leisure time. More and more, as novelty wears thin, developers and marketers will have to provide additional value to the experience. Certainly, one of the directions that theme parks will take will be toward education and entertainment, or "edutainment". Combining the inter-actional and educational properties of modern technology with rapidly improving management expertise will open more windows on the world than Disney ever dreamed of.

Museums, art galleries and archeological sites are being recognized as key attractions for domestic and foreign audiences. Newspapers across China carry listings for a wide variety of State museum and private gallery exhibitions. The range of these exhibitions is broad and growing. A recent Cezanne exhibition in Shanghai drew 4,000 visitors per day. The February 1997 issue of the *China Daily* listed an exhibition of antique carpets from Shanxi and Qinghai provinces, and the Ningxia, Xinjiang and Tibet autonomous regions. The exhibition was held at the Chongwen Workers' Cultural Palace in the district of Chongwen. As well in Beijing, there was an exhibition of ancient coins at the Ancient Coin Museum, and an unusual photography exhibition at the Art Gallery of the Beijing International Art Palace. The exhibition was called "Face to Face". It compared and contrasted the work of a Chinese photographer and a German

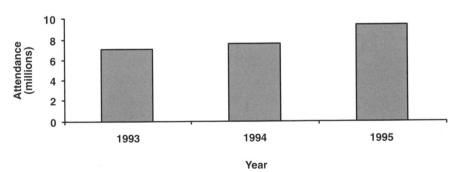

Figure 4.4   Growth of attendance of reading readers at public libraries in China

Data compiled from: China Statistical Yearbook, various years

photographer. Interestingly, the exhibition was sponsored by Siemens Ltd. China — the promotion of an art form that promotes an electronics manufacturer.

These enriched and enriching activities have changed the routes of access to consumer markets. The consumers' needs are different, their tastes are changing and their worlds are expanding.

A nation on the move

There have been a number of forces at work in China to keep people from moving from place to place. The Hukou system labeled individuals as urban or rural and kept them at the same geographic location. Once you had been registered and your place of residence established you stayed put for life. You would be assigned employment at a State enterprise and become eligible for all the benefits the local government might have to offer including medical care and schooling. Essentially, you only existed where and how the Hukou system said you existed. To move or to change employment, cut you off from society and the available social services.

Employment at a State enterprise bound you to that particular factory in that particular part of the country. Advancement within the factory might be possible, but there was little chance of a transfer somewhere else. Essentially, it was employment for life and in exchange for giving yourself over to this system, the State or State enterprise provided housing, pensions, health care and even your children's education.

There was a price to be paid for not being able to move to the best job for your talents or career, or the best city for your health. The consequences to my family were severe. My mother was forced to live and work in Dalian, a northern coastal city. She suffered from asthma which was aggravated by Dalian's severe humid climate. Her health would improve whenever she traveled to Beijing. If we had been able, we would have relocated. The Hukou system made such change impossible. As a consequence, my mother's health deteriorated, and she died prematurely.

State enterprises have also been affected by the economic reforms. In 1986, employees joining State enterprises began to be engaged under contract. By March of 1996, the guarantee of employment for life had collapsed under the pressure of the new market system and 94 million State employees, or 87% of the total, had been converted to contract workers. The government compensated State employees for this loss of security by freeing up residency restrictions and encouraging employees to transfer to jobs they might be better suited for. For many, the change brought only insecurity and anxiety, for others, it meant opportunity and the possibility of advancement.

Contract employment is now fairly standard practice in China. When I was in Urumqi recently I met a young woman of 22, the

Figure 4.5   Workers under contract employment in China

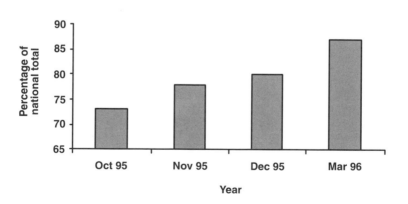

Data compiled from: *Economic Reference News, Beijing Youth News*, 1996

daughter of a friend, who had just begun her first job at a State-owned company after completing studies in international trade. Her mother is a middle school teacher and her father a mid-level official in the local government. She had been born and raised in Urumqi and although only just beginning her first job, she said she was interested in looking for work elsewhere in China. Three weeks after starting her first job the young woman had switched to a job at a joint venture in Zhengzhou, a city in the east of China, almost 2,000 km from Urumqi. A schoolmate had told her about an opening. The young woman took a plane the next day, won the position and has remained there since. This is quite typical of how freely and eagerly the younger generation picks up and moves. It's not that they're capricious, it's that they're drawn by opportunity.

Transportation systems are struggling to keep up with the moving population. On 18 May 1997, the new 2,553 km north–south Beijing–Kowloon Railway opened. The railway provides a direct route for commerce and passenger service from Beijing to Hong Kong. This infrastructure route not only allows greater mobility for the general population, but encourages further development of all the cities along the route. Presently, the train travels at 60 km per hour. Eventually, the speed will be increased to 80 km per hour. Construction of the new railway employed 160,000 workers. They moved a total of 260 million m^3 of earth, dug 150 tunnels, and built 1,110 bridges   all in only three years.

In 1990, China's first superhighway, the 370 km Shenyang–Dalian superhighway opened. Since 1990, more than 3,258 km of superhighway have been constructed in China. China intends adding an additional 900 km of superhighway in 1997. Since 1990, China has built over 100,000 km of highway, bringing the total to more than 1.4 million km.

Presently in China there are over 130 million people on the move. One of the largest groups are farmers who have moved into urban

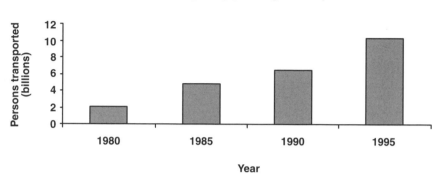

Figure 4.6   China's highway passenger transportation

Data compiled from: China Statistical Yearbook, various years

areas. They have left their farms and a life of relative self-sufficiency and taken jobs in construction, markets and restaurants. Officially, they are still classified as rural, but have become urban and dependent upon the commercial supply of goods and services. Between 1991 and 1995, this group was increasing at a rate of ten million per year. By 1996, their numbers had reached an estimated 100 million; but only 30% of farmers moving to urban areas want to resettle there permanently. Of this group, 70% claim to have moved to urban areas only to make extra money and will return to their original place of residence after a few years or when they have compiled sufficient savings. At any one time, there are 5,000 factories under construction in China's coastal provinces. It is this mobile, shifting workforce that makes such phenomena plausible.

There are some 30,000 hotel rooms in Shanghai. There are 8 five star hotels, 14 four star hotels, 42 three star, 42 two star hotels and 12 one star hotels. Recently, the city government began encouraging the construction of more hotels with a ranking of three stars and lower. Though domestic tourists and businesspeople tend to choose four and five star hotels, the majority of domestic travelers stay in hotels of three stars or less. On any given day in China there are 30 million domestic tourists and businesspeople seeking accommodation. The supply of mid and budget level hotels does not yet come close to addressing this growing number of domestic travelers. According to the China National Tourism Administration, 100 large scale hotels will be completed in China between 1996 and 2000.

Beijing generates one-third of China's total revenue from tourism but suffers a shortage of moderately priced hotels. Currently, there are 40 four to five star hotels in Beijing and 160 one to three star hotels. Nightly rates average US$120–140 at four to five star hotels and US$20–40 at one to three star hotels. Every day 439,000 domestic and foreign tourists pass through Beijing. Presently, moderately priced hotels only accommodate 250,000 guests.

It can also be argued that increased mobility leads to increased portability. If consumers can't move to where the action is, they bring the action to them. Cellular phones, pagers and Walkmans are particularly popular with young people in urban areas aged 18–28.

Figure 4.7   Young people's ownership of Walkmans, 1995

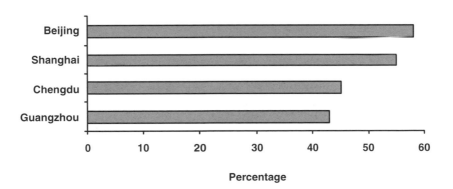

Data compiled from: *Wen Hui News*, 1995

Apartment-bound

Traditional neighborhoods and Si He Yuan housing have diminished greatly in China over the past 17 years. The Si He Yuan is a grouping of dwellings around a square central court. There is a door leading from the Si He Yuan to the Hutong or street. The courtyard is called the Si He Yuan. I grew up in a Si He Yuan that sheltered 12 families. Often, the Si He Yuan sheltered members of the same extended family. This environment allowed a free exchange of information between people with a high degree of trust. There was also a strong sense of physical security as the individual dwelling gave onto an enclosed courtyard that was closed to the street by a gate or door. The shift to modern apartment living has shattered the sense of security, and the comforting contact of trusted family. The nature of life has changed from one of shared living to a more isolated and self-sufficient lifestyle. This change probably creates more emotional discord than physical inconvenience. Telephones and televisions help families and especially the elderly feel connected both to each other and the broader community, but the home has changed irrevocably from being a place to eat and sleep, to a solitary place to live.

The shared existence of the Hutong led to a shared use of many items that are now needed for each individual apartment. The sharing of responsibilities in the Hutong environment made the Si He Yuan fairly self-sufficient, at least in terms of lending a hand at what you did best, in exchange for help with something else.

New housing falls into two categories and has led to a phenomenal construction boom. Working class families now live in apartment buildings of seven stories or less. These buildings rarely have elevators as the building code in China only stipulates elevators in buildings with more than seven floors. The middle class is moving into highrise apartment blocks 20–40 stories high. These buildings emulate Western models and incorporate the elevators into the core construction of the building. These elevators are generally small and in some cases carry a maximum of six.

The Ministry of Construction's objectives for the Ninth Five Year Plan include the construction of an additional 1.2 billion m^2 of urban residential housing between 1996 and 2000. The majority of this housing will be residential apartment blocks.

The move from the Hutongs to the highrise effectively severs the ties between individuals in a neighborhood. The daily personal contact with neighbors and the exchange of pleasantries is gone. In the past, an individual in difficulty or overburdened by work could call on a neighbor to lend a helping hand. The expression *Yuan Qin Bu Ru Jin Lin* (a remote relative is not as helpful as a close neighbor) no longer rings true. Highrise residents are turning more and more to service companies to address their needs.

A 1991 survey of urban Beijing residents found that 72% of residents living in highrise apartments did not know their neighbors' names, 95% had never even visited a neighbor. A fallout of this isolation is an increase in crime, and the higher the apartment building the higher the crime rate. As a result, 57.9% of those surveyed had constructed metal security doors over the existing doors to their apartments, 54.3% had added additional security locks and 21% had installed cat's eye peepholes in their front doors.

Of these urban residents of Beijing surveyed, 21.8% were frightened of being burgled and 20.4% were frightened of going out alone in the evening. Obviously, the growth of security systems and services is inevitable. This presents an additional challenge to door-to-door salespeople, and is perhaps one of the reasons why many direct marketers for goods and services have switched their sales emphasis from door-to-door to relationship marketing, or sales and promotion through friends or relatives.

Figure 4.8   Ownership of security equipment in urban China, 1995

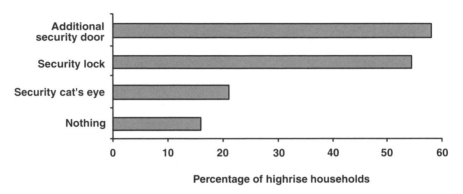

Percentage of highrise households

Data compiled from: Zero Point Market Survey and Analysis Ltd, Beijing, 1995

An additional concern for apartment dwellers is the effect their new lifestyle is having on their health. The Beijing survey showed that illness was more frequent for people living in apartments. Children and the elderly were most profoundly affected as they were the least likely to be able to comfortably and easily go outside for fresh air and exercise. The most profound effect on the elderly is a psychological one as they have moved in their lifetime from a society with numerous and strong social ties, to a life of isolation. It is difficult to measure but easy to predict that depression is a common complaint.

Most of the new 6–7 storey apartment blocks are built without elevators. The elderly or disabled find this a tremendous challenge and often have little option but to remain shut-ins, dependent on the kindness of friends or relatives, or the service companies that have sprung up to address this need.

My friends the Yuans are a senior couple living in Yongan, a small city in Fujian province. As the landscape of the residential housing in Yongan changes, they moved into an apartment building five years ago. Because they tend to get out less and have family and old friends further away, they fill their time by subscribing to over ten newspapers and magazines including *Senior Daily, Health News, Flower Raising* and *Family Doctor*. They also have become avid television viewers by subscribing to cable television and accessing 15 channels. One of these channels offers current share prices on the Shanghai exchange. Others show documentaries, operas, health shows or general education courses.

Children suffer in apartments in China much as they do in the West. There are no convenient public or private spaces for them to play in, traffic around the building is generally busy, and the environment can be dangerous. As a result, their parents buy them toys and videos to keep them happily occupied indoors.

Apartment living is even more complicated and confining for the disabled in China. Generally, apartment stairways are narrow and steep and lifts small, making wheelchair access difficult. Without special assistance, the disabled or ill remain homebound. This isolation intensifies the impact of any disability and often ends up aggravating whatever illness they may be trying to recover from.

Generally, apartment living provides a better standard of living than life in the Si He Yuan. Positive gains far outweigh negative drawbacks. The Chinese consumer is nothing if not adaptable. The isolation and restrictive nature of apartment life has led people to be more concerned with home decoration. Decorative objects such as paintings, photographs, posters and household plants are used to humanize the home environment yet another aspect of China's ever changing economic landscape.

Life for urban residents in China is becoming increasingly active, mobile, and self-contained. This development creates tremendous business opportunities for local and international companies. It also presents new threats to existing commerce as the ever changing environment renders products that are viable today, obsolete tomorrow.

Chapter 5

Luxuries Become Essentials

What they want

What do people want when they have what they need? I started this book discussing the richest man in China, but Larry Yung is hardly a typical mainland Chinese. He is one of the "princelings". His father was close to Deng Xiaoping and remains China's Vice President. He was raised in a privileged environment and completed a university degree. Our interest here is in the evolving consumption preferences of mainland Chinese who have begun to accrue wealth, or disposable income, in the past dozen years. In the 1980s, a very small percentage of the population was part of the market economy and had income to spend. This chapter addresses the huge number of Chinese who have entered the market economy fairly recently, and are now beginning to spend.

Before the economic reforms of the late 1970s had gained the momentum necessary to transform the lives of a significant segment of the population, consumer purchases were confined to the strictly functional. Even if consumers had money, there was nothing, or very little, to buy. What little was available, were bare necessities. If people shopped at all it was for a bicycle, food, or clothing. Clothes came in the "one size fits all" category, and "in any color as long as it's black".

In the late 1970s, as economic reforms took hold and the economy heated up, the new Chinese consumer emerged. Purchases still fell within the realm of the functional, but suddenly, there was lots to buy, and consumers anxious to spend. Many foreign visitors and businesspeople returned from Shanghai with tales of locust-like swarms of Chinese consumers. It seemed the Chinese consumer was prepared to buy almost anything, with little regard to aesthetics or quality. In one Shanghai clothing store, salesgirls were assigned racks of identical dresses. They were the same style and color. The girl would slip into one of the dresses and then wade into the sea of anxious shoppers with her rack in tow. When she emptied her rack, she returned for another, and another and another.

This early period of typically frantic spending lasted from 1978 to 1985, but increasing sophistication, and ever shifting values, soon altered the consumption preferences and patterns of the Chinese consumer.

By 1985, as supplies increased and the novelty of available goods wore off, consumers began to be more discriminating. Quality had become the top concerns in their purchasing decisions. They were increasingly expecting to pay more for better quality. In an effort to address the consumer's new taste for quality, local manufacturers began competing for medals awarded for products of outstanding quality. These medals were awarded at the national level, ministry

Figure 5.1   The evolution of consumer preference

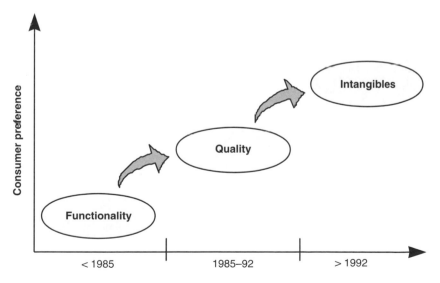

level, provincial and city level, and were used by manufacturers to promote their products. Consumers were making purchases to their own increasingly well informed standards.

In 1992, Deng Xiaoping toured Guangdong province in the south and called for a further opening up of China's economy. Foreign goods and investment flooded into China, and the Chinese consumer finally came of age. The Chinese consumer began to make choices based on more sophisticated criteria, and relatively intangible criteria, such as the aesthetic properties of a product or service. They're certainly intangible compared with the dry practicality of functional purchases, and the limitations of quality driven purchases. Today, if they're looking for material quality, they're also looking for a sense of quality, and the label to go with it. It is not enough to buy the "best", or the most up-to-date and in fashion, it's also important everyone knows about it. This could be carried to odd extremes. Designer suits shipped into China bear large brand labels on the sleeve. In the West, these labels are removed, before people first wear the suits. But in China, particularly at the beginning of this period, young Chinese entrepreneurs, workers and farmers often left them on so everyone knew, for example, the jacket was Pierre Cardin or some other big name designer.

The Chinese consumer has what they need, and with increasing sophistication and intimidating speed, knows what they want. Today, the Chinese consumer makes purchasing decisions based on deeply entrenched social and cultural values, the very same reasons consumers make purchases in the West. The singular difference is the speed at which the Chinese consumer has moved from functionally driven purchases, to intangibly driven purchases, and the high degree of their commitment to these intangible qualities.

There are a number of fundamental areas of concern for today's consumer. Ambience, efficiency, health and status are the most significant. (There were probably similar areas of concern before 1985 and between 1985 and 1992, but they are not relevant enough to warrant separation and discussion here.)

Ambience

Ambience refers to the qualities of an object or activity that are aesthetically, spiritually, or emotionally pleasing. Pleasure, or the quality of the experience, supersedes all other criteria motivating consumer spending.

Obviously, pleasure is highly subjective, and what is visually pleasing to one person may not appeal to another. Consumers in China are spending increasing amounts of their disposable income in search of products and services that are as emotionally and aesthetically satisfying as they are practical, reliable and durable.

In 1995, a consumer survey involving 2,462 urban and rural families selected from 80% of the country, showed that 65% of urban consumers and 52% of rural consumers were prepared to spend more money on products of similar quality but better design. The more education the respondents had, and the higher their income, the more willing they were to pay for good design. The younger generation is more sensitive to aesthetic concerns, and more willing to pay for good design.

Between 1978 and 1995, the national average per capita living space doubled from 4.6 to 7.9 m². With improved housing comes the relatively new concept of privacy. The concept of privacy did not exist when I was growing up in Beijing in the 1960s. It had a very negative connotation and was rarely discussed in the press, or in the literature of the time. Some of this was political, as privacy was seen as bourgeois, some was social, as wanting privacy appeared to undermine the family unit and society. Lack of privacy had more to do with economic realities than anything else. Many generations of the same family often lived together in single room dwellings. Privacy of any kind was impossible. Everything any individual had or did was in full view of everyone else.

Stone walls 2–3 m high on either side of the street, or Hutong, hid family residences from view. Along these walls were doors leading off the street to small courtyards or Si He Yuan. Though the walls lining the streets gave an impression of impregnability, nothing could be hidden from the prying eyes of neighbors. Everybody knew everybody else's business. This lack of privacy was compensated by a very real sense of community and belonging, one I lost when I moved to the West in the 1980s. Modern apartment life in the West left a feeling of disconnectedness and isolation, not knowing who my neighbors were, or what their lives were about. With more and more families moving into highrise apartment blocks, privacy and a disconnection from the traditional neighborhood are transforming the consumer's life.

More and more ads for cosmetics and lingerie are appearing on television, and in popular newspapers and magazines throughout China. Design did not become a factor in the purchase of underwear until the early 1990s. By 1995, 52% of urban consumers and 42% of rural consumers, stated that design was a significant factor in the purchase of underwear.

A growing interest in personal appearance has led to the growth of the cosmetics industry, and a proliferation of beauty salons. There are now over one million beauty salons in China employing some five million people. In April 1995, the first national association of beauty salons was established. Twenty-two provinces, including Beijing and Shanghai, are now in the process of establishing regional associations.

Romance was always a difficult undertaking in China. In the past, young couples would walk city streets arm in arm, or monopolize park benches, to find a place to be alone together. Today, there is more room at home, and a growing number of Western style bars and cafes to visit.

Flower shops have blossomed across the nation, and home delivery can even be arranged through the national postal service. Fresh colorful blooms are increasingly popular as gifts for all occasions. If a friend fell sick and was in the hospital it was customary to bring them fruit or biscuits — today, increasingly, it's flowers. In Beijing, street peddlers sell potted plants for up to RMB 100, and a single rose for RMB 10. One of China's most distinguished women writers, Bing Xin, was presented with 97 red roses on the occasion of her 97th birthday. Wang Zhaoguo, Minister of Political Collaboration, presented her with the roses in Beijing on 4 October 1996, adding, "We are all very happy to see that you are in great health." This might not seem so unusual considering the circumstances but giving flowers as a gift or token of respect withered away in China many years ago. Today, it is a custom that is spreading to all walks of life and all occasions. I visited Dr. Zhou last fall in Beijing. He is a family friend and a very successful doctor. During my visit, there was a knock at the door and two men carried in a huge basket of flowers. Dr. Zhou explained that they were a gift from one of his patients who happened to be a very senior member of the central government.

A fairly new phenomena in China is the sale of sex aids. Sex shops with legitimate business licenses are stocked with all the latest sex aids and contraceptives and can be found in every major city. Recently, I stumbled across a sex shop in Hangzhou, an ancient city of legendary beauty in Zhejiang province. I say stumbled, because there was nothing to indicate that this was a sex shop. In the West, such retail outlets are relegated to certain parts of the city and often have blacked out windows, flashing neon lights, and triple Xs over their doors. This shop looked like any other shop on the street. In September 1996, while waiting for a flight to Kunming, I found sex aids being offered for sale at a counter in the central hall of

Guangzhou International Airport. It seems that these items are so readily available only because the society is still formulating, or re-formulating its concept of privacy, and the boundaries between what is private and what is public. Products, services and, most significantly, ideas are flooding into the country faster than they can be absorbed.

Many of China's s-generation have grown up in apartment buildings. These apartments are generally larger than the homes of the Hutongs and have allowed the only child to grow up having their own room. This is the first generation that has come to expect private space. A 20-year-old cousin of mine in Kunming went so far as to put a large sign over his door reading *Xian Ren Mian Jin*, (Staff Only or Authorized Personnel Only). There is perhaps no clearer statement of the growing desire for privacy, and independence from the family unit, than a separate television for the child. Of course, a second or third television in the home is also a symbol of wealth, and increases status within the community, and if they are large screen color TVs, all the better.

The key decision-making factor in the purchase of televisions used to be quality. Today, reliability and design are the most significant factors. Design becomes a factor in relation to household income. The greater the household income, the more the television becomes a decorative object, chosen as much for its reliability as for how it fits with the rest of the decor. Clearly, television is no longer a novelty, and many families have already upgraded their sets two or three times.

Color televisions are two to three times the price of black and white sets. Nevertheless, more and more households are upgrading to color. In urban areas, the household ownership jumped from 17.2% in 1985 to 89.8% in 1995. In the rural areas, it shifted from 0.8% in 1985 to 16.9% in 1995.

Other forms of entertainment or enlightenment enjoyed in soli-

Figure 5.2 Household ownership of TV sets

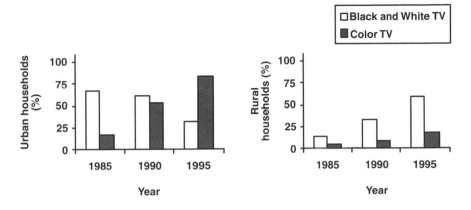

Data compiled from: China Statistical Yearbook, various years

tude include a growing interest in fine literature, and a proliferation of new magazines and newspapers. Western classics by Hemingway, Joyce, Balzac and others, sell out as soon as they hit the book stores. Renewed interest in Chinese classics has led to new editions of the work of such masters as Lao She. In Beijing in 1978, there were only a few newspapers to choose from and most represented the "official" view. By 1994, there were over 233 newspapers in Beijing, most expressing interests far from party politics. In the same period, the number of books appearing on the Beijing market grew ten-fold to 38,498 annually. And by 1994, 1,854 magazines were in circulation in Beijing, six times the number available in 1978. The boom in these goods is related to an increasing interest in expanding horizons, and an improved quality of life. The Chinese consumer, like consumers in the West, searches for meaning and understanding, in a fast moving, ever-changing world.

In cities like Shanghai and Beijing, the search for a richer, fuller life has led many to concerts of European symphony music, and performances of classical ballet. A 1996 survey showed that over 50% had little or no understanding of what they were watching or hearing. A 20-year-old manager of a beauty salon in Beijing says it helps balance the stress of 12-hour days, and thinks nothing of spending RMB 100 each week on tickets to classical concerts, a sum that might represent 7% of her monthly income. One young couple, both doctors at a Beijing hospital, enjoy classical ballet. The young man is attracted by the social and artistic atmosphere, while the young woman enjoys the opportunity the occasion presents to wear elegant shoes and designer dresses.

Though theater goers in the West may have a greater understanding of the meaning of dance and music, they are also motivated by an attraction to the social aspects of the event itself. For both cultures, it is as important to be seen, as it is to see.

Discos, cafes and bars catering to young people, are springing up in every city across China. The average monthly wage is still only RMB 800, but young people will pay RMB 30–60 to enter a disco, and up to RMB 30 for a beer or soft drink, and as much as RMB 80 for hard liquor. They can afford such sums because they live with their parents, and supplement their wages with part-time work. Nevertheless, the amount young people spend at bars and discos is clearly disproportionate to their incomes.

In December 1996, a young friend of mine from Shanghai came to visit my wife and I at our home in Toronto, Canada. Roger (his English name) is a 28-year-old sales manager at an international manufacturer in China. He was in Toronto for two weeks to visit his fiancee. They had toured the local sights, including Niagara Falls. During dinner, they told us they had also visited a new casino just outside the city of Niagara Falls, and that Roger had lost CDN$200 at blackjack. Roger was very cavalier about the money he'd lost, as if he regularly threw away such sums. As they put on their coats to leave, we noticed that Roger was wearing all the latest fashions. He was delighted we cared, and as I reached for a pen and paper, Roger began discussing each item in detail: jeans by Calvin Klein, a sweatshirt by Lee, no frame eyeglasses by Seiko, a vest by Texwood and finally a smashing down-filled jacket by Tommy Hilfiger. Everything he wore had been purchased in China, except for the new Reeboks he'd picked up in the United States. They'd all been made in China, and sold for international prices. Roger added that all his friends in Shanghai dressed in a similar way, and were attracted to similar brand names and accessories. I share this anecdote not only to illustrate the buying habits of a young middle class Chinese, but to show the extent to which the economic boom and international travel have changed their lives.

It is not surprising that travel comes second on the wish list to a better life. For thousands of years Chinese poets and scholars have traveled the country to experience *Qijing*, or nature at her most beautiful. For centuries, poems have been carved into the walls of river gorges to express the visitor's awe at nature's beauty, and many still brave the steep climb and cold temperatures to watch the sunrise from the temple at the summit of Tai Shan, one of the most revered mountains in China.

Today, overseas travel can be arranged through State-owned travel companies or a growing number of privately owned travel companies. From 1980 to 1995, domestic tourism grew from virtually nil to 629 million. Visits to China by international tourists grew from 5.7 million in 1980 to 46.4 million in 1995. Figures from 1995 indicate that domestic tourists spent RMB 137.6 billion, or almost US$16 billion, nearly double the US$8.7 billion left behind by international travelers.

As income levels rise, China's consumers use their weekends for short trips to visit relatives, or to spend time relaxing out of town. In 1995, the 250 km highway between Shanghai and Nanjing opened. Bus companies began service with air-conditioned coaches and

Figure 5.3   What would improve the quality of your life?, 1993

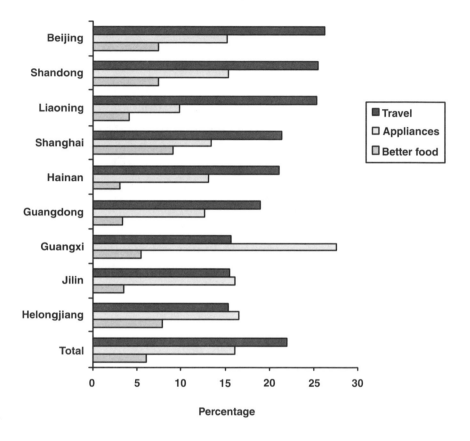

Note: Housing received the highest rating in this survey
Data compiled from: National Center for Youth Research, 1993

airline style attendants. In the first ten days of operation, buses carried 20,000 travelers.

The movement from the Hutongs to highrise flats was the first step away from the secure and socially rich environment of the traditional neighborhoods. The penetration of the family unit by the ebb and flow of other people's lives ceased. Dislocation and isolation are the symptoms of a new society. Consumers are spending more time at home, and increasing amount of money in search of products or services to enrich their new lifestyle. Relieving stress, expressing individuality, and having time of one's own claim more and more of the consumer's disposable income. This movement toward more complex and ephemeral needs can lead to greater sensitivity in interpersonal relationships. Showing hospitality develops personal relationships and expresses greater confidence and status. More and more people entertain friends and associates outside the home, in restaurants, cafes and bars.

Dogs were exterminated during the Cultural Revolution. They ate too much, spread disease, and living quarters were generally too cramped. But the saddest reason for their demise was that they brought joy and enriched pleasure to life; bourgeois ideals anathema to the Red Guard. Today, there are more than ten million pet dogs in China, and they are as much the focus of the family's attention and pride as any single child of the s-generation.

Efficiency

It is about ambience and increased personal pleasure when a consumer upgrades from plain underwear to colorful designer underwear, but it is about increased efficiency or convenience when the same person upgrades their mode of transportation from a bicycle to a taxi, or connects his or her home computer to the Internet. As the income levels rise throughout China, consumers, particularly the young and middle-aged consumers, increasingly favor saving their personal time or energy in trade off with their money.

There is an increasing demand for the products and services that make it possible for the consumer to work longer, harder and more efficiently or conveniently. Consumers are interested in the innovations that enable them to feed and clothe themselves in their increasingly limited free time, and make the most of their private life and leisure time.

One of the most telling incidents that occurred while researching this book took place in one of China's oldest and most beautiful cities, Hangzhou. I was in Hangzhou in the fall of 1995 and took some free time to visit with a cousin. He listened politely and patiently as I described my work on this project. We spent a pleasant few hours together and when it came time to say goodbye he turned to me and asked me for my Internet address. He said it was cheaper than the telephone and just as fast. I was stunned. It felt like a slap across the face. I didn't have an Internet address. I lived in Toronto, Canada, the city *Fortune* magazine calls the best city in the world to live in for business, the most up-to-date and modern. I'd come all this way to study the "emerging" Chinese consumer only to find that even my own cousin had raced past me. This is yet another example of the phenomenal leap-frogging of Chinese consumers. In some cases, the most up-to-date goods are shipped to China a year before they reach the West. When I was in the remote southern city of Kunming, I saw a compact Pentax camera with a 38 mm–160 mm zoom lens. I have yet to see that product on shelves in North America. In North America, in my experience, the compact camera with the longest zoom only goes to 130 mm.

In the 1980s, consumers purchased their food and household goods as the need arose. The idea of shopping once a week was seen as a Western notion. As life speeds up and there is less and less time for anything other than work, Chinese consumers have become weekend shoppers. In a random survey of 300 Beijing families, 64% shopped for their daily needs on the weekend; 25% did their shopping during the week as their weekly break occurred on days other than Saturday or Sunday; and 11% continued to shop as the need arose, often on a daily basis. This group was made up largely of the retired who saw daily shopping as a pleasant way to socialize and pass the time.

As disposable income increases, consumers begin to shop for value added services that will save them time and energy. Quality products presented to their doors by the sales representatives from the successful companies such as Mary Kay meet their needs. The survey of Beijing families indicated that 22% were interested in home delivery, 18% would be prepared to try telephone ordering and delivery, and 14% were interested in joining a membership program that would provide preferred access and discounts to participants.

However, more significant than the move toward convenience shopping is a shift to foods that require less and less preparation.

Frozen foods are becoming increasingly popular in part because they make traditional foods more accessible. Dumplings, wonton, and other dim sum are time consuming to make and generally found in the family home or restaurants. Today, they are mass produced, quick frozen and available in more and more grocers' freezers. Some restaurants have made their dim sum chefs redundant and serve only the frozen product.

Figure 5.4   Shopping pattern of Beijing residents, 1994

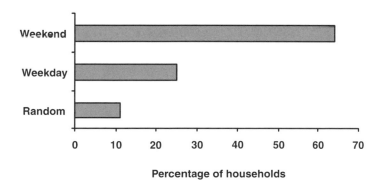

Percentage of households

Data compiled from: State Statistics Bureau of China, 1994

Figure 5.5   Service demands of Beijing residents, 1994

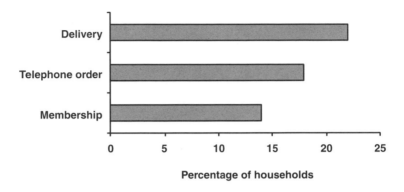

Percentage of households

Data compiled from: State Statistics Bureau of China, 1994

Traditionally, dumplings were a food of northern China. Now that frozen dumplings are available, the delicacy is becoming popular throughout the country. In 1994, per capita consumption of frozen food was only one kg. In Taiwan in 1994, per capita consumption was eight kg, in Japan 12 kg, and in the US 60 kg. If China reaches half of Taiwan's consumption level by the year 2000, the frozen food market will have quadrupled. International companies, such as Green Giant from the US, Birdseye from UK, Bondvelle from France and High Liner from Canada, are already providing a wide range of frozen food to satisfy the stomachs of the Chinese consumers.

In China, *fangbianmian* is the term for instant noodles, but *fangbianmian* means "convenient" noodles, not "instant" noodles. In the West, "instant" describes preparation time; in China, "convenient" speaks of the value of the product — a subtle and interesting cultural distinction reflective of the previous period of consumer development in China.

Convenient noodles have been popular in urban centers and are now making significant inroads to rural consumers. By the end of

1995, there were over 2,000 instant noodle manufacturers in China with 3,000 production lines. A Taiwanese company, Kangshifu, entered the market in 1991, and by 1995 its annual sales had risen to a staggering RMB 2 billion (US$240 million). In 1995, national consumption was running at 12 billion single meal packages per year. Production volume grew 400% from 1990, and by the year 2000 projections suggest national consumption will reach 18 billion packages annually. Market potential remains huge as per capita consumption is still only 25% of Japanese consumption.

In Chengdu, there are a number of companies preparing *Jingcai* (clean fresh vegetables). These companies clean, prepare, pack and then deliver fresh vegetables. Included with the vegetables are leaflets containing recipes and cooking instructions. Three months after opening there were more than 100 delivery outlets for Jiengtsai companies in Chengdu. This is one example of how the expanding service industry in China is addressing the needs of the increasingly busy Chinese consumer.

In 1994, the average annual income was ten times what it had been in 1978, and the population had grown by 25%. In the same period, the annual number of taxi runs in Beijing increased 50 times to over 500 million. Currently, the total number of taxis in the city of Beijing is over 15 times that of the Greater Toronto Area while the population of Beijing is only three times that of Toronto. Of course, the increased number of international tourists and international businesspeople has greatly contributed to this growth. However, most of this increase came from the domestic private sector and is a strong reflection of an increased willingness to spend money for efficiency or convenience.

Private cars are still relatively rare in China and extremely costly to own and maintain. Increasing numbers of people are learning to drive and renting private cars for personal use. By 1996, there were over 50 different car leasing companies across China, and 170 rental companies in Beijing alone.

Ten to fifteen years ago, air travel in China was the domain of international travelers and high government officials. Today, air travel is dominated by domestic businesspeople and travelers. Passenger volume has been growing 20% annually and China is expected to double its civilian fleet by the year 2000.

Figure 5.6   Beijing's passenger taxi transportation

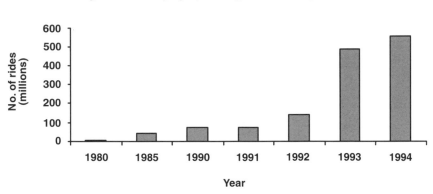

Data compiled from: IMI Consumer Behaviours & Life Patterns Yearbook, 1995

Figure 5.7   China's passenger air travel, by Chinese airlines

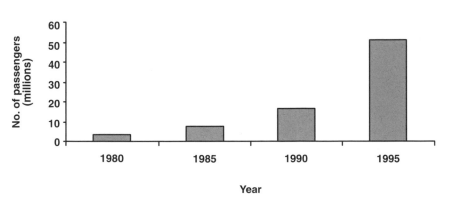

Data compiled from: China Statistical Yearbook, various years

Telecommunications have developed rapidly throughout China. By the end of 1994, in Beijing alone there were over 600,000 pagers in use and 117 paging stations. Along with pagers is a proliferation of communication services including voice mail service, telephone banking and e-mail.

Pagers are perhaps the most obvious symptom of the telecommunication boom in China. Today, pagers do much more than simply page, they have been developed into virtual mini-information centers offering everything from weather forecasts to currency exchange rates and share prices. Young people aged 18–28 have grown up with the technology and accept it as a fact of life. In cities such as Guangzhou, 34% carry pagers.

The personal computer market in China is potentially the largest in the world. In 1996, sales of PCs grew to 1.5 million units, 50% more than total sales for 1995. By the year 2000, sales should reach five million units annually, or US$10 billion. At the close of 1996, 486 processor-based computers dominated the market, with Pentium processor-based computers holding 25% of the market. The PCs

Figure 5.8   China's pagers

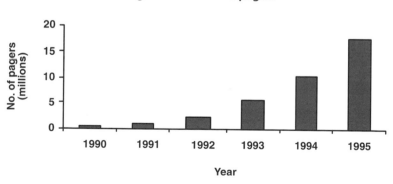

Data compiled from: Yearbook of China's Transportation and Communication, 1996

Figure 5.9   Young people's ownership of pagers, 1995

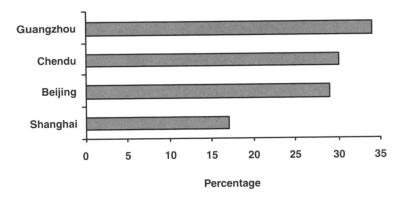

Data compiled from: *Wen Hui News*

purchased for home use have already taken a share of over 20% of the total PC market.

All the major international manufacturers of PCs have entered the China market. There are some domestic manufacturers such as Legend and Great Wall Corporation, but they face an uphill battle against the international giants. The big names, IBM, Compaq, AST, HP, DEC and Acer are all entering the market with their very latest innovations. IBM in particular has experienced phenomenal growth with its sales going from 5,000 units in 1993, to 45,145 in 1994, 87,131 in 1995 and finally 162,000 in 1996. The market is in its infancy and many aggressive newcomers such as Dell, Packard Bell and Tulip are also realizing phenomenal sales growth.

Internet is still in its infancy in China. However it is developing rapidly. Currently all of the 27 provinces and four provincial level cities on the mainland have already hooked up to the Internet. Chinanet, an Internet provider, is owned by the Ministry of Posts and Telecommunications and currently holds 40% of the total Internet accounts across the country. By the end of July 1997, its accounts totaled 110,000 with an anticipated rise to ten million by 2000.

Figure 5.10   Development of PC sales in China

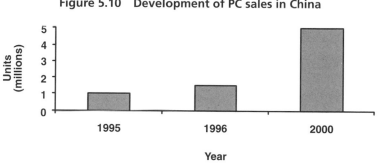

Data compiled from: China Research Corporation China, 1996

Figure 5.11   The development of IBM's PC sales in China

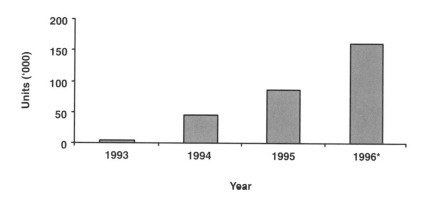

*Estimated figure
Data compiled from: China Research Corporation, 1996

In 1994, the Finnish mobile phone manufacturer Nokia entered the market. By 1996 Nokia had pushed past Panasonic and dominated the market. Nokia and Motorola remain the products of choice for younger people. Nokia's sales continue to grow at a staggering 20% per month.

In 1991, a skilled soldier returned to his home village after his military service, *Tie Jiang Yeng* in Hebei province. Witnessing the economic transformation in the cities, he decided to set up a small telephone switching station in his village. He offered local farmers a telephone connection and switching service for RMB 500. By the end of the year, 16 farmer families had telephones. In the past, villagers had to travel by bus to the nearest city to buy goods, sell products, or get business information. Suddenly, they were connected to the outside world. Very quickly, the village began catching up with the rest of the country. The farmers started to do business over the phone. What took weeks was now taking hours or even minutes. Soon the village became a thriving industrial and commercial center. By the end of 1994, 200 of the 330 families in the village already had telephones in their homes. Multiply this anecdote by millions and the impact of telephones and telecommunications in general becomes clear.

The widespread installation of telephone lines into urban residences only began in 1992. Besides offering efficient

Figure 5.12 China's cellular telephones

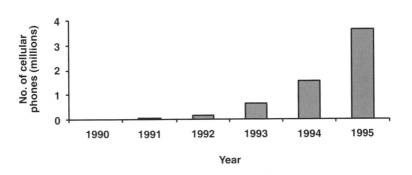

Data compiled from: Yearbook of China's Transportation and Communication, 1996

communication, it soon became an essential lifeline for the whole family. It has made the country smaller by making it accessible. Families can enjoy the comfort and support of relatives living long distances away. Though the installation of a telephone line into the home might cost RMB 5,000, an increasing number of urban families, whatever their economic circumstances, are prepared to pay the price for what they see as an essential service.

Spoilt children become tyrannical rather than charming when they find their voices and the vocabulary to demand more than their doting parents can reasonably provide. But what happens when the s-generation reaches maturity and their parents are no longer around to answer to their every whim? Very quickly they look for services that will do the jobs they're neither willing nor able to do for themselves. Being a spoilt child is not the only excuse; some look for such help because their busy careers leave them little time to clean the apartment, do the laundry, or care for the child. Is this tyrannical? No, but the conditions that lead people to search out such services are.

In December of 1992, the *Economic Daily*, China's *Financial Times*, ran an article called, "When will housework be socialized?" The article referred to the "pot, bowl, dish and spoon symphony" of daily chores and questioned how long it would be before this work would be taken over by service companies. In 1992, a survey in Guangzhou asked what aspect of married life brought the most concern. Of 600 young people questioned, 5% said they were most concerned about being able to afford a nanny. This response was heard more frequently than concerns about an inadequate sex life, or a husband or wife having an affair.

In the early years of the economic reforms most people were simply happy to be able to buy goods that had not been available for decades. If they had any extra money, they usually saved it, but today, extra income is quickly diverted to services that free up the precious time people have when not working.

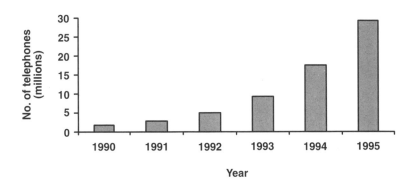

Figure 5.13   China's home telephones

Data compiled from: Yearbook of China's Transportation and Communication, 1996

In Beijing, service companies are expanding to accommodate every imaginable need. If you want to move, you call Li Kang Ltd. If you want cleaning services you call San Xining Cleaning Company. Shanghai companies offer skilled workers who provide care services to the elderly and the young. In Nanjing, you can find companies to do your laundry, deliver your lunch, or send someone to your home to teach you a new skill. In Chengdu, there are companies ready to cut and prepare vegetables and deliver them to your door, and florists with home delivery. You can pick up the phone and hire a casual worker, often a university student, to come to your home and complete whatever chore needs attention.

In 1992, a national survey of urban residents conducted by the Chinese National Union found that on average, men spent two hours per day on household chores, and women spent 3.2 hours on household chores. If only half the urban population decided to reduce their household chores by 20%, or one hour per day, and hire someone to do this work, the market for household services would be 100 million working hours per day. This would create an eight hour per day full-time employment for 12 million people. Even though this market would be worth RMB 150 billion (almost US$20 billion), it remains largely unexploited.

In December of 1995, a grocery store in Taiyuan called All Season Fresh Produce began a monthly purchasing program. The idea was to help provide fresh groceries to people whose work schedule made shopping difficult. The customer would place their order for fresh produce which would then be delivered every second day. A 5% discount was offered to those joining the program. In the first few days of the program sales averaged RMB 200. Two weeks later sales volume had increased 500%. After three weeks a total of 892 families had joined the program.

As the pace of life quickens and time becomes increasingly limited, more and more products and services will be needed to assist in the efficient organization of social and family life. Chinese society will become increasingly dependent on service companies as the pressures of life increase and the companies expand into every aspect of daily life. A vicious circle, or yet another opportunity in China's burgeoning market place?

Health

If you were asked what you wanted most, what would it be? Happiness? Beauty? To be famous and powerful? Where would you rank good health? Most of us would choose differently at different times. Emotionally, wealth might be the attribute of choice, but rationally, good health is the safest bet, for with good health comes long life and many more years to reach all your goals. In China, the cultural significance of good health and a long life is profound. The Chinese revere the old for what they've done, and for the wisdom they believe age brings. Chinese consumers today are turning with increasing interest to products and services that improve health, and open the door to a longer and more productive life.

Nutritional analysts in China believe 20% of the population to be healthy. Only 20% of the population feels their complaints are serious enough to seek medical attention. The rest of the population treats illness or discomfort primarily by changing their diet, with traditional medicines, and increasingly, with ever more prevalent Western style over-the-counter (OTC) drugs. This will create a self-medication market of 600 million people — a market twice as large as the population of the United States or of the European Union.

Obviously, the consumer's perception of what is healthy has a tremendous impact on the food industry. A survey by the State Statistics Bureau showed quality and hygiene to be the top criteria when purchasing food. Quality came first for 73.9%, and hygiene for 60%; only 24% said price was a key purchasing criteria. The more attention consumers pay to their health, the less concerned they are about price.

Figure 5.14   Food purchasing criteria of Beijing residents, 1994

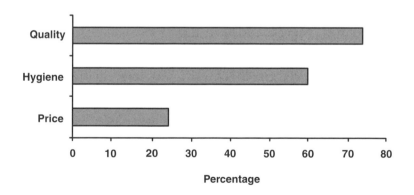

Data compiled from: State Statistics Bureau of China, 1994

The national managing director of a successful foreign supermarket chain in China explained to me in early 1996 that frozen food is becoming increasingly popular because of its convenience, and a perception that some frozen foods are more hygienic than their fresh counterparts. Meats that spoil easily, like seafood and chicken, or processed foods or meats, are increasingly popular frozen foods. It is not that Chinese shoppers are naive, they are quite shrewd. It is just that frozen foods have proven to be generally fresher and therefore more hygienic than the same products sold fresh in open stalls or grocery stores.

The make-up of the Chinese diet is changing. Generally, it is a move toward higher nutrition. The daily per capita consumption of meat soared 81% between 1982 and 1992. Egg consumption rose 200%, and dairy products were up 300%. Grain consumption fell by 10% in the same period.

By 1995, the average urban Chinese was consuming 36.1 g of fish, 78.3 g of meat and poultry, 24.2 g of dairy products and 76.1 g of eggs daily.

Along with frozen food and processed food comes an increasing demand for fresh food. Improved transportation and infrastructure make it possible to ship fresh food and produce to the farthest corners of the nation. From 1985 to 1993, in Guangdong province in the south, consumption of traditional staples declined, with per capita daily grain consumption falling 31%, and pork falling 4%. Fresh food, or a greater variety of fresh foods, have filled the gap with per capita poultry consumption up 72%, fruit increasing 35% and vegetables up 17% during the same period. As grain consumption falls, consumers are shifting from low quality rice sold in bulk, to brand name packaged rice.

A new phenomenon in China is the emergence of fashionable health foods. Today, consumers' attention is being drawn by three color groups: red, green and black. Red foods include carrots, sweet potato, red beans, red rice and tomatoes, etc. Green foods fall into two sub-categories. The first green foods are those foods raised in a biologically friendly environment and regulated by a government authority. This can include "green" meat, "green" vegetables and even "green" processed food. The other green foods are those that are naturally green in color, green vegetables and fruit, etc.

Black foods are considered the healthiest. These foods include black beans, black mushrooms, black grains, black sesame, and even seaweed and kelp. Black rice is believed to improve kidney function and is also good for pregnant women. Black sesame is prescribed for digestion, circulation, and milk supply for lactating women. Black beans are good for reducing high blood pressure, improving the health of the heart and preventing arteriosclerosis. They are also prescribed to enhance sleep and general good health. Because these foods are black, and believed to be healthy, they are often sold for 50–100% more than comparable items.

During the war, and time of famine, people often turned to wild grass, plants and bark, for nourishment. Curiously, in these times of growing prosperity, these items are now beginning to appear on the menus of five star restaurants. There are even restaurants in some larger cities that specialize in wild grass cuisine. The reason that these restaurants are popular is the consumers' increasing sensitivity to healthy food and the belief that these wild grasses are healthy because they are grown naturally and without artificial fertilizers. They are also believed to have some "gensanic" magic power if only because they are wild.

Thousands of years of dependence on traditional Chinese medicines encourages this trend toward "green" or "wild" products. It has also been a factor in the consumers' increasing demand for these foods. Naturally grown foods, foods without artificial color or flavoring and reduced sugar content are becoming increasingly popular, as are wild grasses and game. As of 1994, there were over

200 companies in China producing some 400 different kinds of green foods. A survey by the Ministry of Agriculture of 48 food manufacturers, manufacturing 62 different green foods, showed that between 1991 and 1992, the profitability of these companies increased 80%, while production increased 17.1%, with sales up 24%. The trend toward green foods has led the government to establish regulatory offices in 26 provinces and cities across the country.

The market has also shifted from one product for all, to segment specific products. Not only is the market segmented for children, young adults, middle-aged and elderly, it has also segmented into health specific concerns. Many different products are tailored for improving general health, longevity, increased brain energy, beauty, weight reduction and improved sexual ability. Presently, there are over 3,000 companies supplying health enhancing food products in China. By 1996, the market for such products had already passed RMB 30 billion (US$3.6 billion) in off-factory prices.

Carbonated drinks were extremely popular in the early 1990s. Increasingly, the more sophisticated consumers are searching out natural beverages, including nutritious fruit juices and bottled mineral water and distilled water. Natural juices must come without artificial sweeteners or coloring and they must be free of additives for preservation. A wide range of fruit juices are popular with Chinese consumers including carrot juice, apple juice, orange juice, tomato juice, peach juice and green tea. To address this growing trend, Coca Cola Corporation China recently developed the *Tian Di* series of natural drinks with its local partner in China. Canadian juice maker Lassonde Group, entered the market on the strength of this trend alone. Lassonde has become one of the most successful international beverage companies in China, and has achieved higher than Western market price margins and double digit growth since its establishment.

There are some four million families living in Shanghai of which 300,000 families use bottled mineral water, or bottled distilled water for drinking. To offset the high cost of bottled water the government has begun to build outlets that use standard equipment to purify the water at each location. These outlets are only 60 m² in size and are located primarily in residential areas. This water is 40% cheaper than bottled distilled water, and a family of three need spend only RMB 20–30 for a month's supply of drinking water. According to the government's plan, there should be 50 water outlets in Shanghai by the end of 1996, and 100 by mid-1997. The service will be available throughout Shanghai by mid-1998. A total of 4,000 outlets will be opened in other parts of the country in the same period.

There is also a growing trend toward natural fabrics in clothing. Artificial fabrics, and the chemical processing involved in their production, cause allergic reactions in many. Consumers are increasingly aware of the health benefits of natural fabrics. Silk and cotton breathe, and are much more comfortable in both hot and cold climates. Manufacturers have begun producing anti-allergy clothing with brand labels such as Nature's Call, Country Life and Green Nature.

Clothing design is undergoing significant change. Confining designs are giving way to *Xiu Xian Fu*, clothes of less rigid design, supple and comfortable to wear. Consumers are changing their clothing more frequently than ever before. In the past, it was common to wear one set of clothes from morning to night. Today, at the end of the day, the office worker removes shirt and tie or dress and slips into something more comfortable for his or her well-deserved rest.

The increased sensitivity to a healthy lifestyle has led to greater demands on the health care system. Consumers have begun to search out the doctors and hospitals with the highest reputation for quality service. Many hospitals have developed "doctor of choice" programs. Consumers can choose the doctor they wish, or go to a hospital other than the one they might normally be assigned to. They are prepared to pay a premium for this service that might be 10–50 times higher than the standard price. One post-operative patient explained, "Choosing a well-known doctor to do the operation was worth the extra money because it made me feel more at ease. I wasn't so frightened getting on the operating table. I felt at peace, that I was in good hands."

Consumers now have the resources and are willing to pay for child care, elderly care, at-home nursing services and general medical attention. Today, throughout the country, many experienced doctors and dentists with reputations high enough to attract clientele, are leaving hospitals and setting up lucrative private practices.

The pharmaceutical industry in China has been growing at an average annual rate of 20% since 1990. This is in striking contrast to an average annual growth of 7–9% in the US and Europe during the same period. The total pharmaceutical market in China (including traditional medicines) is expected to jump from RMB 88 billion (US$10 billion) in 1994, to RMB 200 million (US$23 billion) by 2000. Of these figures, the market for Western medicines is expected to grow from RMB 63 billion (US$7 billion) to RMB 150 billion (US$17 billion). The market for Western medicines should reach US$60 billion by 2010, and should become the largest market in the world by 2020.

Figure 5.15   Medicine consumption by country, 1994

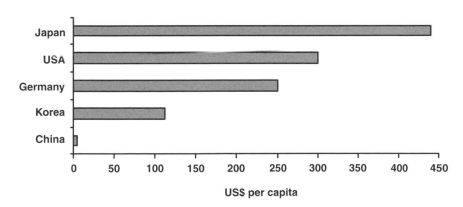

Data compiled from: China Pharmaceutical Yearbook, 1995

Figure 5.16   Western medicine market in China

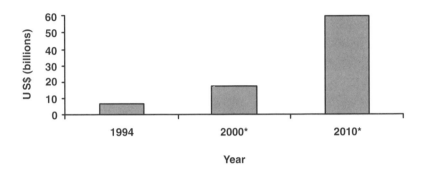

*Estimated figure
Data compiled from: State Pharmaceutical Administration of China, China Pharmaceutical Statistics, Deloitte Consulting, 1996

China continues to import more and more Western medicines to meet growing demand. Imported medicines can range from the esoteric, to popular drugs like Johnson & Johnson's Tylenol. Increasingly, large international companies are establishing manufacturing bases in China. From 1988 to 1995, the number of international joint ventures for pharmaceuticals and medical devices jumped from 26 to 1500.

Western medicines are not replacing traditional Chinese treatments, in some cases they are serving as a compliment or back-up. Chinese health tonics continue to be the leading preventative medicine. Traditionally, this was a market for the elderly, but more and more consumers of all ages are being drawn to Ginseng products, medicine liquors, pearl powder and other, even more exotic tonics.

Traditionally, the Chinese have treated mental distress through the body, with acupuncture, massage or herbal tonics as well as some Western medicines. More and more, they are turning to psychology and psychiatry for help. In Beijing, a hotline for students of middle

Figure 5.17   China's import of Western medicine

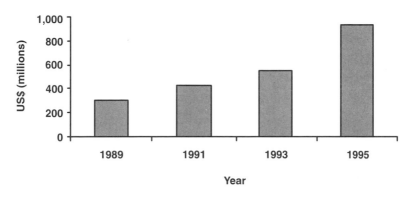

Data compiled from: China Pharmaceutical Statistics, Chinese Industry and Commerce Press, 1996

and primary schools was set up to deal with students suffering psychological problems due to stress. By 1992, 10,000 students were calling this number annually.

Tai Chi and other *Qigong* exercises (similar ancient disciplines of physical movement and meditation) are traditional methods for physical conditioning and meditation. Today's consumer is either too impatient, or has too little time, to devote to learning the complicated movements of these disciplines. They're looking for a quick fix, a fast track to physical fitness. Exercise salons and home exercise equipment are becoming increasingly popular. My cousin, a journalist in Beijing, uses her rowing machine almost every evening to unwind and keep fit. A young factory worker I met with a monthly income of RMB 500 told me he had spent RMB 3,000 to buy a treadmill for his home. Treadmills are particularly popular with the elderly. A recent survey showed that 30% of families would like to have exercise equipment in their homes. A sporting goods center in Dalian reported that equipment sales increased 100% from 1994 to 1995. The most popular home equipment ranges in price from RMB 2,000 to 6,000.

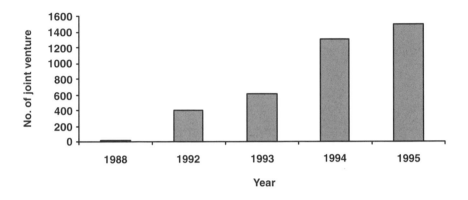

Figure 5.18   International pharmaceutical joint ventures in China

Data compiled from: China Pharmaceutical Statistics, various years

Health and fitness clubs are growing in popularity, and there is an increasing focus on organized public sports. In 1994, in Guangzhou, 200,000 residents were members of health clubs or spas. The cost of a single training session is often less than RMB 5. Body building is also on the rise with 200 magazines devoted to the sport. Monthly circulation exceeds 20 million nation-wide.

Status

Status has a greater influence over consumers in China than it does over consumers in the West. But how can status be relevant in a "socialist" country ruled by a communist government?

In the broadest sense, status means the same in the East as it does in the West: to be seen to be of the highest order or rank and receive the greatest respect. The difference between status in China and status in the West begins with the definition of the individual, and the individual's place in society. In the West people revere the rebel. The rebel is the outsider challenging the status quo. Their existence is justified by their own action instead of by other people's view. It doesn't matter if he or she wins or loses, the point is that they stand up and declare themselves different, and not part of any group. For example, James Dean is this mythical hero personified.

In China consensus rules. The individual is important, and to be different is important, but it is being different within the parameters of a certain group. For our purposes here we will call it interpersonal-based individuality. Status is much more subtly expressed in China than in the West because the individual only ever exists in the context of one group or another. Their existence is justified by the view of the people surrounding them. Children strive for greater status among their friends in the neighborhood with better toys, bikes, or clothes, but the criteria changes according to the group. A bicycle might help status in the street, but it takes a Walt Disney logo or a Mont Blanc pen to increase status at school or in the office. Of course, similar distinctions exist within groups in the West, but in China, the only way status can ever be expressed is in the context of the group. Of course, my purpose here is to explain that there is a much broader base and higher commitment of status driven purchasing in China than Western business strategists might realize.

Figure 5.19   Comparison of social value

China vs West

China		West
Status (Chinese style)	_____	Status (Western style)
Interpersonal	_____	Individual
Life extension	_____	Life of today

There are other significant cultural differences between the East and the West that affect the definition of status in China. In the West, people espouse the "just do it" mentality. People live for now, for today and damn the consequences. In China, almost everything is decided according to long-term goals. At a very young age, children are already being told to make an effort for their future, to go to university, to become a scholar or an entrepreneur.

Daoism and Buddhism are the most prominent religions in China. Both emphasize meditation and encourage the notion that through meditation anyone can become another Buddha or Dao Master. Millions meditate even though they have little hope or real expectation of becoming another Buddha. This struggle for perfection is about the process, not the end result. This idea permeates the psyche of the population and explains the 16-hour days students spend at their studies. It also means that people in China are willing to suffer and fight for goals that need longer time, more patience and harder work.

To a certain extent, Chinese society is obsessed with extending or preserving life. In ancient times, when an individual of means died, detailed ceramic replicas of all their worldly goods would be buried with them to help them in the afterlife. The old are revered in part because of how they have defied the passage of time. The idea appears in long-term cross generational planning. Every generation tries to raise the family's status and reputation in society. Distinguished careers and graduate degrees raise status, and the higher the status, the longer the family or individual will be remembered.

Wealth is the most significant determinant to status in Chinese society today, followed by power and knowledge. Status-oriented purchases are all geared to getting the consumer higher up the rung of wealth. The poorer the consumer, and the lower the level of education, the greater the proportion of their income spent on status-oriented purchases. Unlike the West, what you see is what they own.

Credit is not readily available in China, consumer purchases are generally made with hard-earned cash, earned by themselves or at least by their extended family.

Generally, education increases the individual's opportunities for wealth, and therefore status. But there was a short period of time in the 1980s when people began to doubt the importance of education. *Xiahai* is a verb meaning to plunge into the sea, and is a common term used to describe those that had plunged into the market economy. All those who could be described as having *Xiahai* were making more than those still involved in the socialist system. A shoe repairman in the streets of Beijing could make three times the salary of a university professor. However, this period didn't last too long, and opportunities began to narrow for all but the best qualified. A 1995 survey of urban residents of Beijing and Shanghai, shows that income levels are now commensurate with education level — the greater the education, the higher the pay.

Consumers from all walks of life recognize that education is one of the most fundamental routes to increased status. Seminars are being organized by local authorities so farmers can be kept up to date on the most recent agricultural innovations, and many skilled professionals are continuing their education at night schools. A survey of farmers near Shanghai indicated that 50% had participated in various skills and technology training. Over 80% said they wanted to send their children to university. Da Zhong Si village, a suburb of Beijing, became extremely prosperous as a result of the organization of a large market for fresh produce. A farmer from the village claims to have hired 12 different tutors for his children, and has spent over RMB 10,000 toward their education in recent years.

But it is the young children who receive the most attention, and upon whom the most pressure is placed to succeed in school. Many parents hire tutors to augment regular primary school instruction, and often send their children to music lessons and computer courses.

This can be a considerable financial burden as one 45-minute piano lesson can cost from RMB 60 to 80.

Parents are also willing to spend huge sums of money to transfer their children to schools with high reputations. In Beijing, it can cost up to RMB 20,000 (US$2,400) to transfer to a superior primary school, and over RMB 50,000 (US$6,000) to transfer to a better middle or high school.

Many parents feel the best contribution they can make to their child's education is to buy them a personal computer. Of course, many parents in the West feel the same way; the difference is in how the children use their computers. In the West, children play computer games, in the East, they are seen more as tools for learning.

In Beijing in 1994, an employee of a clothing company told me he had spent RMB 6,000 to buy a computer with an Intel 386 processor for his teenage daughter. He also enrolled her in a word processing course. He said, "I don't expect her to become a computer expert, but I do believe computer skills will be essential for survival in the twenty-first century. It's like reading, you don't need it all the time, or even do it for a living, but you need to be able to do it when necessary." A senior manager said, "I decided a long time ago that by my daughter's eighteenth birthday she needed, one, a driver's license; two, to be able to use a computer; and three, to understand commerce and accounting." He said he was convinced that success in the future depended on mastering these skills.

In 1994, a survey of 400 families from the eight districts surrounding Beijing showed that 5% of households had personal computers, 7.8% had electronic learning devices and 11.1% had manual typewriters. Of these families, 23.7% had pagers and 30% telephones.

The lower the grade at school the higher the individual expenditure. In primary and middle schools, students are primarily brand consumers. They wear clothes by Benetton and shoes by Nike and Reebok. Name brand bikes are also important. Parents will pay up to RMB 300 for brand clothing, but as much as RMB 1,000 for popular mountain bikes. In Beijing, mountain bikes are twice as expensive as standard bikes but have 25% of the market. Their popularity is so great it is anticipated they will have 50% of the market by 2000. School stationery has to be designed by Disney. Primary and middle school students from working class families spend up to RMB 300 in pocket money per month.

High school students in China are not unlike teenagers in the West. Clothes and parties are critical for status. In 1996, the average high school student was spending RMB 200–300 per month on entertainment and snacks. Housing, food, clothing, tuition, books and transport are not included in this sum. In working class families, 50–70% of the family's total income is spent on the single child. A working class family in Kunming has an average monthly income of RMB 1,200.

Many purchases are competitively motivated. If your neighbor has a 20-inch television, you must buy a 24-inch set. This applies to motorbikes, cameras, sports equipment and computers. In Kunming, my cousin spent RMB 42,000 (US$5,000) for a motorbike. He is single and has been working for three years. These motorbikes are called "sharks". The most popular were the black sharks but today consumers like my cousin will pay a premium for a red one. They can afford these kinds of purchases because they live at home until they marry and can spend their personal income on themselves. Of course, the prime reason for their purchase is to make the owner feel special, and part of an elite group.

Luxury items in China are generally purchased for status and not because of the consumer's sophistication and taste. Martell brandy and Cartier lipstick are not necessarily enjoyed for their aesthetic qualities but because of the effect they have on others. In Southern China this competitiveness goes to odd extremes. Farmers in small villages compete with each other to build higher and higher homes. One farmer built a seven storey house, the height of the average apartment building in the city, for only his wife and two children.

Years of isolation left Chinese consumers relatively unsophisticated shoppers. They trusted brand names, and paid more for foreign goods simply because they were foreign. As they have been exposed to more and more selection, and greater quality, they have become selective and fickle. Today in Beijing, consumers can choose from more than 100 different brands of foreign and domestic skin care products, and over 70 brands of shampoo. There are an astonishing 300 brands of toothpaste, and 400 varieties to choose from country-wide.

Consumer purchasing is increasingly value driven (price sensitive). As competition in the marketplace intensifies, domestic and international companies will have to offer both the tangible and the intangible qualities consumers want at competitive prices.

Many firms had early success simply because they were the first. But being first, or carrying a strong brand name, is no longer a guarantee of success. China has an extremely fast-changing consumer market, with a growing segment of status-oriented consumers. Many well-known Western fast food chains offering chicken, burgers and fries are popular in China today not because the food is better than anything else available at local fast food outlets, but because young people perceive these well-known Western shops as being the coolest place to be. When fads shift, will they fall behind?

Chapter 6

As For The Necessities

Shifting priorities

Chapter 5 showed how rapidly the Chinese consumer is becoming increasingly sophisticated. It also explored the interests and influences behind consumer spending. This chapter focuses on the total impact of the background, shaping forces and emerging trends onto the individual consumer and the family unit. What does the individual do with their income? How is the household income divided up? What do they spend it on, how much do they spend, how much do they save, and how? These are essential issues and evolving priorities.

We move from the broad motivating factors behind consumer spending to the specific needs of the individual consumer and the family unit in this fast changing society. What are today's necessities and how will those goods and services change in coming years?

The individual cares first and foremost about family and home, but investment and insurance are becoming significant expenditures. The child's education and telecommunication needs remain high priorities.

Home improvement

An Ju Le Ye is an ancient Chinese adage that means success will only come after one's home is settled. A home, or a place of one's own, is a common wish for people in every culture, but in China it takes on greater significance. In fact, it's not uncommon for people in China today to go to extreme lengths to save enough for a down payment, including starving themselves, or risking malnutrition by eating only instant noodles. Companies wanting to attract the most skilled employees are compelled to offer quality housing as part of a compensation package.

Today, and for at least the next decade, the consumer market in China will be driven by the housing industry. This will include new construction of private residential housing and the renovation or upgrading of existing residences. The prevailing secondary markets will be in household furniture, appliances and home decoration. These purchases will be for new residences, or purchases made to upgrade existing equipment. In most established urban families, major appliances are now at least ten years old. Many intend to upgrade their appliances only after purchasing a home of their own. Recently, the *Asian Wall Street Journal* carried a story on a 46-year-old resident of Guangzhou Mr. Bi who remarked, "I'm not buying another new appliance until I own my own home, preferably without stairs."

Certainly, one of the motivating forces behind this mass drive toward home ownership is the ability of the population to actively purchase and own a home. The Chinese population, for the first time in many decades, is now allowed to own property. With ownership comes pride. People now have the impetus to care about the condition and upkeep of their homes. Pride of ownership drives the home renovations and household appliance market. If it is yours, then you make it the way you want it, and keep it in good working order.

Traditionally, the State concentrates its resources on three to five pillar industries. These industries may range from telecommunications to natural resources to infrastructure. Until recently, the automotive industry was one of the pillar industries. Strategists believed that the economy would be driven by this industry as most people would buy cars as soon as they had the means. But by late 1996, evidence that the housing industry was a prime force in the economy was so overwhelming that the government was forced to change its strategy and begin to focus its energy and attention on the housing industry. Policies are now being formulated to direct resources toward this sector. Not only does this show how different China's consumers are from consumers in the West, it also shows that government policy is being decided by the consumer, not the bureaucrat.

Foreign firms cannot enter China thinking that they can change the tastes or habits of China's consumers, certainly not if the Chinese consumer has become so powerful that they can change government policy.

In 1994, for the first time in the history of China, the total average annual per capita spending on food dropped below 50% of income. This speaks of the general rise in income levels and standards of living. It also suggests other priorities have emerged for the Chinese consumer. With the commercialization of housing and the move toward improvement of the home environment, more and more of the consumer's resources are being directed at housing or housing related expenditures.

In July 1996, a survey conducted in Beijing, Dalian and five other major cities in China showed that low income residents are more concerned about health care reform, and higher income residents care more about housing reform. Income levels were also a significant factor with 75% of those with a monthly income below RMB 300 concerned about health care reform. 75% of those with monthly income exceeding RMB 1,000 were concerned about housing reform. As wealth increases, so does the desire for, and pride in, a home of one's own. The survey also showed that the issue was age sensitive with those over 50 generally more concerned with health care reform and those under 50 concerned with housing reform. In the survey, concern about inflation ranked third behind housing and health care reform.

One of the features of the new China is a shifting of responsibility for the individual's welfare from the State to the individual. In this spirit, State companies are now moving to privatize accommodation that was once offered as an employee benefit.

Presently, accommodation provided by State companies or subsidized by the government costs 5–10% of the occupant's disposable income. By 2000, as State enterprises and organizations transfer even more responsibility onto the backs of the individual, the actual cost of housing is expected to take at least 15% of disposable income. As this shift continues, and housing takes more and more of a bite out of income, the consumer will be forced to cut back on luxuries or expenditures he or she may now take for granted.

Figure 6.1   China's total residential housing rental market

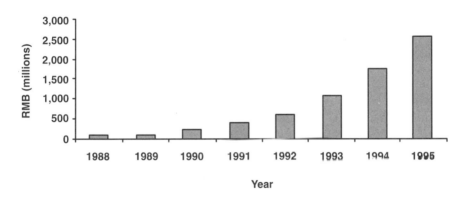

Data compiled from: China Statistic Yearbook, various years

In the city of Shenzhen, in Guangdong province, the average per capita income increased five-fold between 1987 and 1995. During the same period, the cost of housing increased eight- to nine-fold. In 1996 in Shenzhen, the average per capita expenditure for housing was RMB 448. This sum represented 15% of total monthly expenditure. An examination of the rental accommodation available at the time showed that even lower end commercial rental housing cost RMB 900. Clearly, an average family supported by a single wage earner would be spending more than 15% of their monthly expenditures on accommodation.

The cost of rental accommodation becomes less economical the deeper it eats into the family budget. In Chengdu, between 1978 and 1996, the per square metre cost of rental accommodation increased 1,200%. State employees, and workers in the private sector are starting to buy their accommodation from their employers, or on the open market. Private property appeals not only to traditional values, but as a hedge against the new tyrannies of inflation and market demand.

According to the *Chengdu Construction News*, there are six categories of housing available for purchase by urban residents in China. The most expensive housing is built by commercial developers and is only accessible to those with a relatively high standard of living. Low profit government controlled commercial housing is available to a broader range of middle class consumers of moderate means. Non-profit housing, *Jingjishiyong* housing, is only available to government employees and employees of State-owned companies. Another form of non-profit housing is *Anju* housing. This non-profit housing is also only available to low income government employees and employees of State-owned companies and is designed to meet the most basic needs of the occupant. Finally, there are two categories of subsidized housing. The first subsidized housing is only available for poor families with certificates attesting to their penury. The other subsidized housing is created from converting rental premises into privately-owned housing.

In 1995, the average per capita living space of urban residents in China was 7.9 m^2. During China's Ninth Five Year Plan, 1.2 billion m^2 of new urban housing will be constructed bringing the per capita living space of urban residents to 9.0 m^2. During the same period,

Figure 6.2 China's total residential housing sales

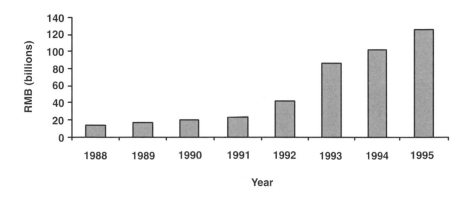

Data compiled from: China Statistical Yearbook, various years

rural housing is expected to grow some 3.0 billion m². Every year until 2000, 600 million m² of rural housing will be constructed and 6–7 million rural families will move into new housing. Every year, 240 million m² of urban housing will be constructed moving 4–5 million urban families into newly constructed or reconstructed homes.

But new housing is not the only concern. In 1996, a total of 33 million m² of housing was in dangerous condition and need of complete renovation. In 1996, surveys revealed that 3.25 million urban families lived in houses or apartments with 4 m² or less of per capita living space. To improve the living conditions of lower income citizens, the State has been renovating some 20 million m² of residential housing annually. As a result, 500,000 families enjoy newly renovated accommodation each year. The combined figures of all newly constructed housing and all renovated housing indicate that up to 12 million urban and rural families are moving into new homes each year.

From 1978 to 1994, 100 million of China's 280 million rural families moved into new homes and by 1995, the average per capita living space of rural residents had reached 20 m². In 1995, the total amount

Figure 6.3 China's residential housing built

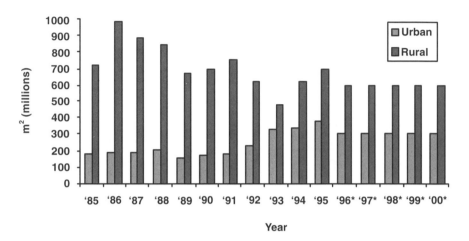

*Estimated figure
Note: Urban housing space includes renovated/upgraded housing space
Data compiled from: China Statistical Yearbook, various years

Figure 6.4 China's residential housing renovated by State entities

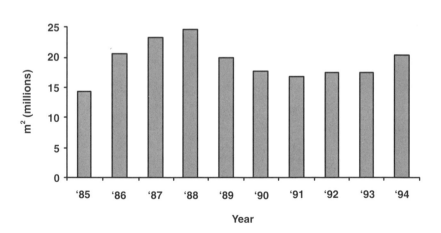

Data compiled from: China Statistical Yearbook, various years

spent in China on the purchase of residential housing by rural and urban private residents reached RMB 47 billion (US$5.5 billion). This figure does not include the amount of money spent by individuals constructing their own residents.

This insatiable demand for residential housing has led to significant international joint ventures. In 1996, CITIC Real Estate, an arm of China International Trust & Investment Corporation (CITIC), and Beijing East Lake Real Estate signed an agreement with ING NV, a diversified financial group from the Netherlands, to form a joint-venture company to develop residential housing. Many other international joint venture have also been established to seize opportunities in the residential housing market in China including Beijing Chengxin Real Estate Development Co., Ltd which aims to renovate and develop the old residential housing in the Dongcheng county of Beijing, and Dongguan Xiegang Dahou Industrial Construction Co., Ltd which specializes in developing and managing low cost residential housing for average employees, etc. International construction companies already established in China have now begun to shift their focus from construction of hotels and office buildings to apartment construction and the renovation of existing residential housing. Perhaps more significantly, both domestic and international firms are shifting from high end residential housing targeted at expatriates or wealthy Chinese, to middle market and lower end residential housing.

From the air, most of China's cities seem dominated by construction cranes and scaffolding. In Shanghai alone, an estimated 20% of all the construction cranes in the world are engaged in highrise commercial and residential construction. But not all of the residential housing sells quickly. Some remains empty because income levels have not yet reached the level where such purchases can be maintained. At the end of 1995, a total of 50 million m^2 of commercial housing was ready for occupancy but remained unsold. Between 1980 and 1995, the square meter price of residential housing increased

Figure 6.5   China's residential housing by private purchase

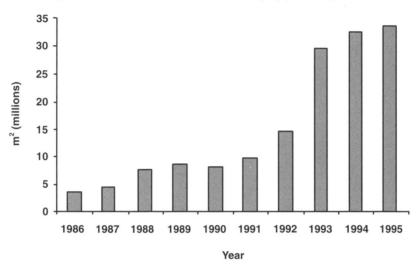

Data compiled from: China Statistical Yearbook, various years

Figure 6.6   China's commerical residential housing sold

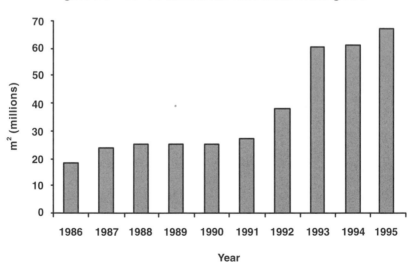

Data compiled from: China Statistic Yearbook, various years

1,500%. During the same period, average incomes increased 1,000%. This disparity must be reduced to bring customers to the finished product, and to avoid seeing the construction boom turn into a bust.

Before 1996, high government taxes pushed the price of housing beyond the reach of the general public. Almost 80% of the cost of building came from government taxes including levies on the cost of leasing land. To boost the housing market across the country the government has reduced taxes levied on home construction. These measures should reduce the cost of basic housing by 50–60%. Guangzhou plans to lower the tax and non-tax cost of development by 25%, Zhongshan by 30%, and Zhuhai has offered to cut all taxes to a maximum of 7% of total construction costs. As a result, the price per square meter for urban residents with moderate income in provincial capital cities should not exceed RMB 1,000, in mid-size cities it should not exceed RMB 800. Larger cities such as Beijing, Shanghai and Guangzhou, however, will struggle to keep their price per square meter below RMB 2,000.

Adding fuel to both the construction boom and private residential ownership are developments in the banking industry. In April 1996, Construction Bank of China extended the length of the mortgages it offered from three years to ten years. The Commercial Bank of China also extended housing loan eligibility to anyone with legal residency, extended its mortgage length to ten years, and extended the mortgage limit to 70% of the total price of the residence.

In the past, developers in Beijing sold to overseas Chinese and foreign expatriates. Recently, their market has shifted to domestic Chinese. In order to secure their new market, and adapt to the means of domestic consumers, they have lowered their price per square meter to US$1,000. The managers of three apartment buildings that came on the market in the third quarter of 1996 advised that 70% of their sales were to domestic Chinese. Of course, they were bought by affluent domestic Chinese. With total savings of some RMB 4,700 billion, banking reforms, and the continuing rapid growth of the economy, more and more of these purchasers are expected to come from middle and lower income buyers.

If the first step is one's own home, then the next step is a home like no other. Very few people buy a home without deciding how they will change it before they move in. This can range from a coat of paint to major renovations. Improvements continue in response to changing needs and rising incomes. The natural companion to China's current housing boom will be an increase in the purchase of household appliances, and products related to home decoration or enhancement.

For the past few years, an average of 100,000 families have moved into new housing in Shanghai each year. In 1995, the average cost of home decoration for each of these new homeowners was RMB 10,000 (US$1,200). From 1994 to 1995, the sale of home decoration materials grew 50%. Average spending on home decoration is even higher in Guangzhou. In 1994, the average working class family spent an average of RMB 10,000 per household, but a family headed by a well-paid employee with a university degree might spend RMB 30,000–40,000 for home decoration.

The overall market for interior decoration in China has grown from RMB 8 billion (US$1.5 billion) in 1990, to RMB 60 billion (US$7 billion) in 1995. By 2000, the market is expected to reach RMB 200 billion (US$24 billion). As a result of the rapid growth of this market the number of interior decorating companies in China has grown from 10,000 in 1990, to over 40,000 in 1995.

The overall increase in the number of family units in China is growing at a faster rate than the population. From 1980 to 1994, the population grew 19.2%. In the same period, the number of family units grew 45.4%. More and more young people are leaving home to marry and set up homes of their own. This trend will increase as more of the s-generation reaches maturity.

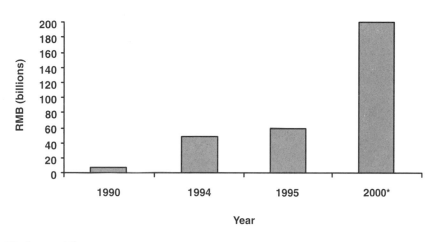

Figure 6.7 Home improvement market in China

*Estimated figure
Data compiled from: *Market News*, 1996

A recent survey showed that 58.9% of all young people surveyed stated that their first priority was the improvement of their home environment or a home of their own.

Investment and insurance

People spent freely in the early days of the economic reforms. Rents were low and health care and education almost free. New-found cash went on fine clothes, food and entertainment, and all the new consumer goods and services. But as the reforms spread, and the economic boom took hold, long-term planning replaced carefree spending. The shifting of responsibility for individual welfare from the State to the individual caused many to reassess their spending priorities. Perhaps it would be wise to look into additional health insurance, and what about life insurance and a pension plan? How do you protect yourself against inflation and job loss? Or finance a home or a child's education? How do you accommodate the shifting priorities the different stages of life bring? These questions, and the industries that address them, are leading to an increasingly sophisticated banking and insurance industry in China.

China has one of the highest per capita savings rates in the world. Presently, 85% of all families in China choose bank deposits as a means of preserving wealth and fighting inflation. The notion of using wealth to generate wealth is acceptable in China, but is still only conceivable to a relatively small minority of the rich. For the majority, the most immediate concern is still to make ends meet, and assume the challenge of the daily responsibilities once shouldered by the State.

In 1978, total deposits were RMB 21 billion. By 1986, funds on deposit had reached RMB 223.7 billion, and by 1996, that figure had soared to RMB 3,500 billion (US$420 billion). If cash, foreign currency deposits, stocks and bonds are combined, the total liquid assets of the Chinese people rises to RMB 4,700 billion (US$550 billion). The rate of growth for these savings is impressive in itself with total liquid assets growing from RMB 3,000 billion (US$360 billion) in 1993, to RMB 4,000 billion (US$480 billion) by 1995. Urban residents had the highest rate of savings with an average per capita savings of RMB 10,000 (US$1,200).

As savings increase, people begin to look for better and better ways to put those savings to work. When the Shenzhen stock market opened in July 1991, 1.5 million investors arrived with cash in hand to buy stocks. A 1996 survey in Guangzhou, showed that 700,000 residents, or one out of ten, had invested in the stock market. One-third of those investors had only entered the stock market in the previous 12 months. Initially, the stock market was a game for entrepreneurs or the rich, but increasingly, salaried employees,

Figure 6.8 China's total private deposits

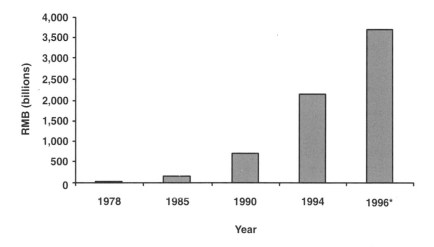

*Estimated figure
Data compiled from: State Statistics Bureau of China, various years

teachers, doctors, professors, even average workers, are all becoming interested and active analysts and investors.

High saving rates are not new to China but have been instrumental in fueling the economic boom. In 1994, more than 80% of China's capital needs were met by domestic sources. By the end of 1994, the total market capitalization of A shares on the Shanghai stock exchange had reached US$30 billion. The total market capitalization of A shares on the Shenzhen stock exchange reached US$15 billion. In 1994, the combined total trading volume of A shares on the Shanghai and Shenzhen exchanges reached US$95 billion, with most of the investors being domestic Chinese. One reason for the rapid growth of China's stock markets is certainly the lack of attractive alternatives for personal/private investment.

By the end of 1994 the Shanghai stock exchange had 550 members, and the Shenzhen stock exchange 496 members. Both exchanges

Figure 6.9   Wealth preservation choices of Beijing residents, 1995

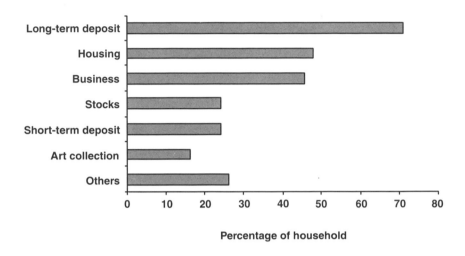

Percentage of household

Data compiled from: Statistical Bureau of Beijing, 1996

offered direct trading access from more than 25 major cities across China.

Security firms and financial institutions have followed the rapid development of the stock exchanges. By the end of 1993 there were 87 security firms in operation, and 400 non-specialized financial institutions engaged in securities trading (including trust and investment companies as well as investment banks). The number of local branches of security brokers throughout the country grew to 3,000. Chinese investors could do their trading through these local brokers, or on the two nation-wide centralized systems of STAQ and NET.

The growth of the Shanghai stock exchange between 1991 and 1995 was staggering. The number of listed stocks grew 600%, its members grew 2,100%, trading volume grew 1,181,000% and the total number of investor accounts increased 6,600%. By mid-1996, the Shanghai stock exchange boasted nine million investor accounts.

The Shenzhen stock exchange had six million investor accounts. Of the nine million investor accounts on the Shanghai exchange, more than 75% were held by people living outside the city limits of Shanghai. By April 1997, the number of investor accounts on the Shanghai exchange had already reached a staggering 15 million.

Though there is the interest and the infrastructure for investment, investment choices for the general public in China are still very limited. There are no private banks or mutual funds and most bank accounts offer very limited options or benefits. By the end of 1995, there were approximately 575,000 bank branches and other credit outlets in China. This made the cover rate reach 2,100 persons per branch and outlet. Inter-branch banking is still very limited. Electronic banking is developing rapidly and by the end of 1995 an electronic interbank system connected 400 branches in major cities across China.

Figure 6.10   Number of bank branches in China, 1995

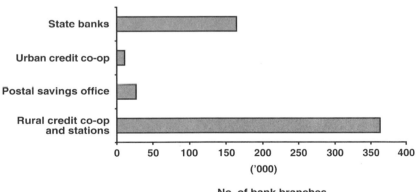

No. of bank branches

Note: The number of foreign banks branches was 166 in 1996
Data compiled from: China Statistical Yearbook, 1996

Investors in China have few options. Bank deposits offer interest rates lower than the rate of inflation, and investing in the stock market remains risky and difficult for the unsophisticated. Currency trading or investing on the international financial market is still impossible. The most attractive investment for the average investor is government bonds.

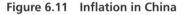

Figure 6.11   Inflation in China

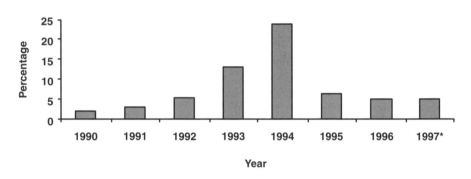

*Estimated figure
Data compiled from: China Statistical Yearbook, Chinese Ministry of Finance, various years

At this point in their economic development the Chinese are saving more for future consumption than the accumulation of wealth. They are putting money aside for housing, their child's education, care for elderly parents, or emergencies. There is a tremendous need for investment opportunities that will satisfy these priorities and offset the effects of inflation.

The most reasonable option open to most citizens, besides bank deposits, are government bonds. Since 1981, the Chinese Government has sold RMB 500 billion (US$60 billion) worth of government bonds.

A growing category of investors are the s-generation who continue to live at home after completing school and entering the job market.

Figure 6.12   Average wealth preservation pattern of
Chinese household, 1994

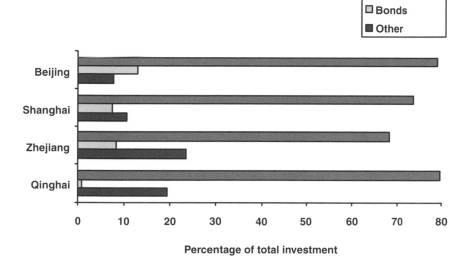

Data compiled from: State Statistics Bureau of China, 1994

Figure 6.13   Urban 18–28 year olds' monthly savings, Shanghai, 1995

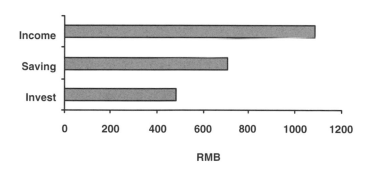

Note: Investment is part of saving
Data compiled from: *Wen Hui News*, 1995

They have a high level of disposable income because their parents and grandparents continue to cover their basic needs. A 1995 survey of Shanghai's urban young people between 18 and 28 showed that 20% worked for foreign invested companies. Their average per capita monthly income was RMB 1,085 and their average per capita monthly savings were RMB 710. This savings rate of 65% is significantly higher

Figure 6.14   Rural residents deposit rate, Shanghai

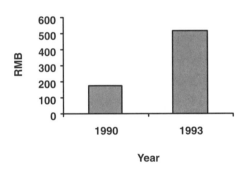

Data compiled from: *Wen Hui News*, 1994

Figure 6.15   Rural residents deposit rate, Shanghai

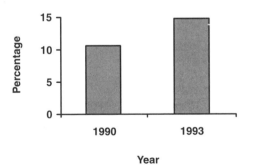

Data compiled from: *Wen Hui News*, 1994

than China's overall average; of their monthly savings, 44% is directed into specific investment vehicles.

The deposit rate for rural residents is beginning to rise. In 1990, rural residents living on the outskirts of Shanghai retained an average of RMB 177 on deposit, or 10.7% of their average annual income. By 1993, their annual deposits had grown to an average of RMB 518.98 per person per year, or 14.9% of their annual income.

China's banking system is still relatively closed to foreign participation, but pressure from major trading partners and China's own wish to join the World Trade Organization is placing pressure on such restrictions. Many government officials feel that the only way for China to modernize its banking and investment services fast enough to meet economic conditions and growing demand, is to remove restrictions entirely. By 1996, change became apparent with 26 major cities beginning to open up to foreign banking participation. By the end of 1995, 137 foreign banks had been given permission to set up branches in approved regions conducting approved business activities.

With health care costs on the rise, China is in need of a comprehensive insurance system. From 1990 to 1995 the total annual expenditure on health care by State employees more than doubled from RMB 16.37 billion to RMB 35.15 billion.

The insurance business in China today is dominated by two domestic firms. In 1995, the People's Insurance Company collected premiums totaling RMB 47.6 billion, representing 79.12% of the total market. The Pacific Insurance Company collected RMB 6.6 billion for 11% of the total market. Together, these two domestic firms control over 90% of the insurance market in China.

In 1995, China's total insurance market reached RMB 60 billion. Total life insurance premiums were RMB 20 billion. By 2000, the market is expected to grow an additional 200% to reach RMB 200 billion.

In the early 1990s it was rare to hear much talk of insurance or

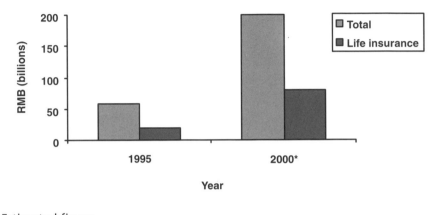

Figure 6.16   Insurance market in China

*Estimated figure
Data compiled from: *China Daily*, Deloitte Consulting, 1996

even notice the presence of insurance companies or agents. Today it seems you can find a table set up to promote insurance policies at every street corner and in every market. They offer insurance policies ranging from general health insurance, hospital care insurance, pension insurance, unemployment insurance, accident insurance and life insurance. To accommodate the doting parents of the s-generation, many offer Child's Life Long Happiness insurance. This is a policy designed to provide the child with an income supplement. The purchaser pays RMB 360 annually until the child reaches age 14. From age 15, the child then has the option of drawing from a total of RMB 170,000 in payments until age 65. It's a hugely successful policy and represented 80% of all policies sold in the early 1990s.

The spread of the insurance industry into China's western regions is being hampered by the lack of skilled professionals. In 1994, the per capita premium payment in Shanxi, Shaanxi, Gansu and Qinghai provinces, and the Ningxia Muslim Autonomous Region was

US$2.80. But in the east, in Shanghai, Jiangsu and Zhejiang, the per capita premium payment was US$7.20. Qin Daofu, a former president of China's top insurance company, the People's Insurance of China, has suggested that provincial authorities in the west send select candidates to actuarial courses at eastern institutions. Other industry experts have recommended the establishment of a center for training insurance professionals in Xi'an, Shaanxi or Lanzhou, as these provinces are home to major electronics and aviation industries, both of which are major clients for property insurance.

Presently, there are 110 million people in China over 60. By 2000, that number should climb to 130 million. Older people have recently begun to purchase road safety insurance in response to an increase in road accidents. Many older people have been killed while on their way to shop or out for a stroll. In 1995, 2,146 were killed while riding a bicycle and 4,741 were killed while walking. In July 1996, the Pacific Insurance Company and the China Road Safety Association began issuing road safety insurance. As of December 1996, the policy was available in 88 cities and was selling extremely well. Buyers of the policy can purchase from one to twenty units. Each unit costs RMB 10 and provides compensation of RMB 3,500 (US$421).

A typical example of the success insurance companies are having can be seen in the example of Pingan Insurance Company. In 1995, the company's customer base grew by almost 50,000, pushing its private premiums to RMB 70 million. During the 1996 Chinese New Year celebrations in Beijing, Pingan set up 100 mini-counters in market streets. From February 17 to March 4, they sold 5,500 insurance policies with total premiums of RMB 2 million. In little more than a year its sales force has grown from 100 to 2,000. Over 95% of all new policies are sold by sales representatives at mini-counters in market streets.

Insurance companies have also begun to send their sales agents door-to-door. In 1994, the American International Assurance Group started a door-to-door campaign in Shanghai. Initially, residents resented the intrusion and often stuck up signs warning insurance agents to keep away. But the practice of door-to-door sales has now become more familiar to the residents if not commonplace and agents are met only with the skepticism of seasoned shoppers.

The Chinese Government has been aggressively promoting insurance. In August 1996, the village of Dazhai was hit with severe rain and flooding causing RMB 8 million in damage. Insurance companies quickly paid out compensation to local policyholders. This persuaded those who had been skeptical before the flooding to purchase policies of their own. The village had been a model village during the time of the rigidly planned economy, one of Mao's ideal villages. Now, ironically, it is an aggressive pioneer in assuming responsibility for its own destiny, as almost all the residents have purchased property and health insurance.

By the end of 1995, 87 million urban employees had joined a basic pension plan. This represented 75% of all urban employees. This number should grow to include 80% of all urban employees by 2000. Today, only 20% of rural residents participate in pension plans. It is hoped that this will increase to 30% by 2000. Pension plans are a major concern as today only 22.4 million retired people are covered by pension plans.

By the end of 1995, 80 million employees from 530,000 State enterprises had joined unemployment insurance plans. By early 1997, 1.55 million participants have received unemployment benefits.

Today, there are 26 insurance companies in China whose total premiums reached RMB 60 billion. A number of international companies have received licenses for operating within certain specified regions in China; another 70 international firms have applied for licenses. In anticipation of a further opening up of business, more than 150 international insurance companies have set up representative offices in China.

International insurance companies are also drawn to China's potential investment market. One of the world's largest insurers, AXA / National Mutual Corporation, has established an investment fund in China. The goal of the fund is to raise US$500 million, 70% of which will then be invested in China's high-tech industries. As an expression of their commitment to the region, AXA / National Mutual Corporation has donated US$600,000 to train local Chinese for the insurance business, and for local cultural and sports activities. Recently, this included a company sponsored three-day table tennis tournament.

In November 1996, China's first life insurance joint venture was established. Zhong Hong Life Insurance Co. Ltd, China National Chemical Import and Export Corporation (Sinochem) and Canada's Manulife Insurance announced initial registered capital of RMB 200 million (US$24 million). Industry observers say the joint venture will bring advanced foreign management expertise and experience to China's still young insurance industry. Manulife International Ltd. continues to direct its operations in China, Hong Kong, Taiwan and Macao from its regional headquarters in Hong Kong. Presently, Manulife has offices in Beijing, Shenzhen, Shanghai, Chengdu and Guangzhou.

Education and telecommunications

Education is important in China. Of course, the clearest indication of how important the individual sees education is in how much money he or she is prepared to spend on it. Statistics confirm the increase in the family's total expenditure on education. If the cost of school supplies and increasing tuition and extra tutoring is added, the numbers are higher still.

From 1992 to 1994, in Jinan, a medium-sized city in the Jiaodong Peninsula, the average amount of money spent by an urban family on education for their child increased at an average annual rate of 22.02%. The family's expenditure on books alone increased 50.16% annually during the same period.

A 1992 survey of 360 families in Beijing showed that 66.3% of total monthly expenditures went toward the single child. A 1992 survey of 700 primary school students in Beijing revealed that 158 had their own electronic keyboard, 49 had an accordion, 9 had a classical piano and 251, representing 36.3% of the total, had attended special music lessons. When the survey focused on students in the first grade, 47.2% were found to have taken special music lessons.

Tuition to regular schools is increasing each year. And the competition to proceed to higher levels forces many parents to send their children to enrichment courses or expensive private tutors. Entry into some of the better schools requires parents to pay entrance fees of between RMB 10,000 and 60,000 annually, which does not include the costs of books and supplies. Presently, a first grade pupil carries up to 20 books to and from school each day. The actual number of books students are obliged to read in any given year now equals the total number of books students might have read over several years before current reforms began. The cost of books and stationery alone is a huge burden for most families. The survey conducted in Jinan showed that the average annual expenditure for stationery for children grew 33.65% between 1992 and 1994. In Beijing today, 10% of families were saving specifically for their child's education.

Education costs do not stop once the child enters university. If the child is successful, and is one of a small percentage to enter one of China's universities, parents are faced yet again with ever-increasing costs. By the end of 1996, two-third of China's colleges and universities, or a total of 661, had begun charging tuition. By 1997, most of the colleges and universities are expected to start charging tuition. By 2000, all college and university level students will be obliged to pay tuition. Even if a child is exceptionally gifted and is selected to be sent to study in a foreign country, the burden continues. The family, parents and child are obliged to sign a loan contract with the China Scholarship Council to cover the high expenses of overseas study.

An MBA degree is becoming an important qualification for entry into foreign or domestic firms. But a good wage and a bright future may seem little compensation for the sacrifices the bearer made to get it. Often, MBAs are self-financed and acquired under a part-time program involving night school classes completed at the end of an already long and arduous day.

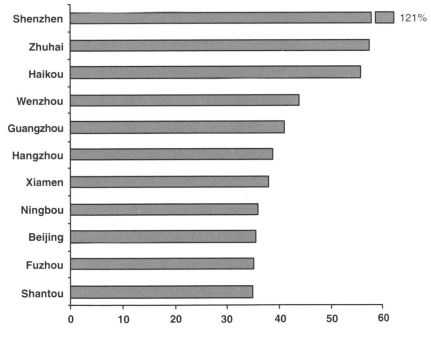

Figure 6.17   Selected leading cities for residential telephone ownership, 1995

Percentage of households

Data compiled from: Yearbook of China's Transportation and Communication, 1996

By 1995, 17% of urban households in China had telephones. By 2000, the percentage should rise to 30–40%. In 1995, there were a total of 57.6 million corded telephones in the country, by 2000 this number is expected to triple to 174 million. By 2010, China should have the largest number of corded telephones in the world at 420 million. Cellular phones are growing at an equally impressive rate. In 1995, there were 3.6 million cellular phones in China; that number should jump 400% by the year 2000 to 18 million cellular phones.

In 1995 alone, 12 million corded telephones were installed, two million cellular phones connected, and seven million new pagers activated.

Social changes are fueling telephone use in China. As life becomes more compartmentalized, and more and more people move from traditional neighborhoods to highrise towers, the need to connect with

Figure 6.18   China's residential ownership of mobile phones and pagers

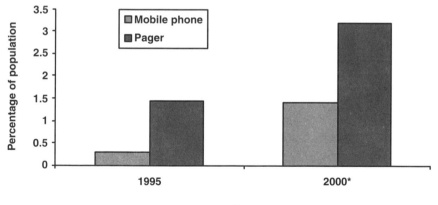

*Estimated figure
Data compiled from: China's Ninth Five Year Plan for Economic and Social Development and the Targets for 2010, 1996

friends and family increases. The percentage of total expenditures dedicated to the purchase of telecommunication products and services is increasing rapidly. The telecommunication sales volume of the Chinese Post and Telecommunication Service increased 500% between 1991 and 1995, with sales going from RMB 13.41 billion to 73.27 billion. Between 1995 and 2000 total sales are expected to double.

Figure 6.19   China's telecommunication market

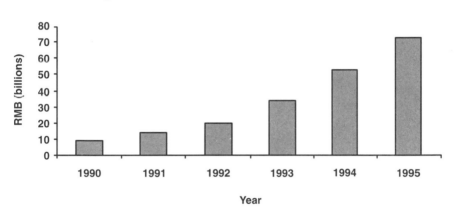

Data compiled from: Yearbook of China's Transportation and Communications, 1996

As the economy develops, consumers become increasingly rational about their spending habits. Savings, insurance and pension plans will begin to draw more and more money leaving less available for casual purchases. This phenomena has left some department stores with flat sales growth, or a decline in sales volume. From 1992 to 1994, the national ratio of total annual retail sales to total annual savings declined from 4 to 2.5. By 1996, the total private savings on deposit reached a staggering RMB 3,500 billion.

A 1995 survey of 30,000 urban families gives a strong indication of the shifting priorities of the Chinese consumer. The average per capita expenditure on both taxis and telecommunication rose 120% between 1993 and 1994. The average per capita expenditure on medical products grew 92.5% during the period, with Chinese medicines and health tonics making up 30.2% of the growth. Expenditure on adult education grew 52.3%, and spending on

Figure 6.20   Distribution of spending by urban residents

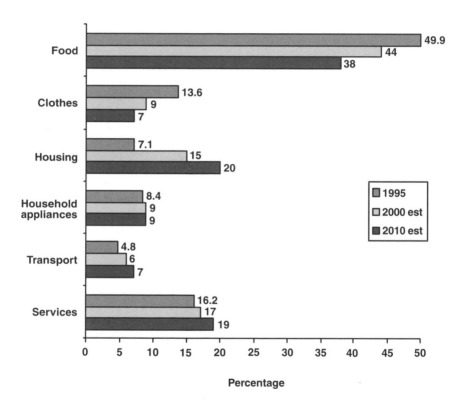

Note: Food includes liquor, tobacco and beverages; housing includes water, electricity and fuel; household appliances include durable goods and daily articles; transport includes communication; and services include education, health care, culture and entertainment

Data compiled from: China Statistical Yearbook, Journal of Beijing University, Consumption of Chinese People by 2000, analysis of Deloitte Consulting, 1997 textbooks grew 39.7%. Expenditure on clothing grew only 8.8%. Spending on interior decoration grew 63.5% between 1993 and 1994 and spending on general housing renovations grew 58.5%. Total average per capita spending on housing made up 6.8% of total household spending in 1994.

Money for impulse purchases or casual spending is declining because the government is withdrawing more and more subsidies on items that were once inexpensive or free. Gone are the days when monthly rent cost the equivalent of a pack of Marlboro cigarettes, or a child's annual tuition no more than the price of a McDonalds hamburger. This pushes consumers toward more rational spending, making them more value driven and price sensitive. No longer will consumers spend half a month's salary on a night out, or two year's salary on a color television set.

Generally, spending is becoming more and more rational. The growth of higher range consumption will slow as fewer people move from low income levels to higher incomes. China will also come to see a greater polarization between the haves and the have nots. One of the most significant shifts in the retail market will be the expansion of discount retailers and private label products. There will also be a new phenomenon to contend with, a new consumer category to explore the DINKS (couples with double incomes and no kids).

Chapter 7

Taking
The Plunge

Taking the plunge

"You cannot wait for things to settle down and become clear. That day may not arrive for a very long time, if ever." These words, spoken by Mr. Lee S. Ting, Asia Pacific Managing Director of Hewlett Packard Inc., describes the situation for companies that are considering a market entry into China and companies that are considering a market expansion within China.

Every new era or social movement is illuminated by an idiosyncratic language. Key words come to define an age. Swing, cool, hip, bobby soxer, hippies and yuppies define generations, times and even attitudes. In the early 1980s, as the economic reforms began to take hold and prosperity spread, an expression came into use in China to describe those individuals who had decided to abandon the old ways and venture into the new uncharted waters of economic reform. A colleague might resign from a secure position at a State enterprise saying he was going to help his brother-in-law with a new privately-owned fish farm. Everybody would shake their heads and say warily that he'd *Xiahai* or "plunge into the sea", and entered the market economy. (*Xia* means plunge into, *Hai* means the sea.)

The expression colors the action with risk, and those that took the plunge in the early days were certainly seen to be taking a chance diving into new uncharted waters. Those early adventurers were seen as rebels who were risking more than the security of State employment. Today, the term implies commitment to the market reforms that have transformed China. Those that are now taking the plunge are seen as contributing to the new market system. However with over 180 million people now working at non-State-owned enterprises across the country, they're no longer the exception, they're the rule. It also serves well for the title of the final chapter of this book, and an encouraging battle cry for all businesses entering the China market.

The international business community regarded companies entering China in the early days as foolhardy, because China's economic stability seemed in doubt. Unfortunately, there is no colorful phrase attached to those early pioneers. In spite of general skepticism, many entered, and risked considerable sums to do so. Two examples that quickly come to mind are two joint-venture large scale luxury hotel projects built in Beijing in the early 1980s, the Jianguo Hotel and the Great Wall Hotel. The international community was particularly skeptical about their success because of the generally long recoupment time of large scale luxury hotel projects. The degree of their concern was unwarranted, as both hotels have recouped their initial investment several times over and continue to thrive. Today in China, according to the Swisshotel Management Group, the recoupment time for such hotel projects is only ten years, at least half the international average of 20–25 years. International businesses now entering China are seen as farsighted, not foolhardy.

Previous chapters have outlined many of the key consumer trends and their associated risks in China's new economy. Obviously, these trends present tremendous opportunities for businesses interested in this dynamic market.

Here a brief overview of major business issues and options for business strategists interested in the China market is presented as well as unique information on current trends for businesses already operating in China. The chapter is organized into four main headings, Approaches in practice, Keys to success, Challenges ahead, and outlooks for Staying on top.

Approaches in practice

The essential ingredient for success in the China market is to focus on one specific niche. Four generic niche approaches have been applied in the China market by both domestic and international companies. Figure 7.1 maps out two different sets of strategic options. One applies to businesses already established in the market but who wish to expand, the other is for businesses entering the market.

Figure 7.1   Approaches in practice

Business expansion (already active in the marketplace)	Market entry (not yet active in the marketplace)
Product-niche approach	Product-niche approach
Geo-niche approach	Geo-niche approach
Consumer-niche approach	N/A
Value-niche approach	Value-niche approach

Product-niche approach

The idea is to target the market with a well-conceived product or service and to push it to all possible geo-markets and customer segments. In this situation the product's advantages — both tangible and intangible — must be clearly differentiated from those of its competition. The product may be an entirely new product, or a completely revised version of an existing product. Pharmaceuticals often fall into this category.

Advantages: Companies that can clearly differentiate their products or services from others will have a significant competitive edge. It is the most powerful option for companies entering a market place rich in product choice and categories and where marketing campaigns by competitors are highly aggressive.

Disadvantages: The rapid diffusion of knowledge, and the constant creation of new ideas, makes it increasingly difficult for companies to develop any product or service that is truly different from any other. Benefits may be short lived for those companies lucky enough to develop unique attributes for its products. As soon as the new product enters the market place, competing products begin to absorb and adopt its uniqueness. Companies may be able to enter the marketplace with this approach, but once established they may have to explore other approaches to maintain positive growth.

Geo-niche approach

In this situation, a company targets a geographic region with a substantial but unfulfilled demand for products or services that are already available elsewhere. This is an approach generally taken by smaller companies. They quickly become the big operator in a small market before others have identified the potential. Big operators can also enter these markets early to ensure long-term dominance in the overall market. The best historic example of this is the American retailer Wal-Mart.

Advantages: This approach allows smaller companies a chance to establish themselves in a market place without overwhelming competition. Fewer resources are required to begin operations. The smaller company has time to get a firm foothold before the surrounding economy in the region becomes significant enough to attract major businesses. Additionally, local governments in underdeveloped regions are more sympathetic to new businesses and offer incentives for entering the market place. In larger centers such as the Shanghai region it is survival of the fittest with little opportunity or space for smaller companies to enter.

Disadvantages: Less developed regions often have lower purchasing power and less developed business infrastructure. As a result, strategic planners must pay attention to a broader range of concerns and be prepared to commit more time before realizing significant returns.

Consumer-niche approach

A company identifies a consumer segment with a significant demand and brings its product or service to that particular segment. Companies using this approach usually have highly identifiable personalities and identities and target the same consumer segment with a broad range of products throughout widespread geo-markets. The Walt Disney Company is a good example of this kind of company. The company has been active in China for a long time and provides a broad range of products for children.

Advantages: Companies using this approach rely on a strong synergy between individual consumers within a consumer segment, as well as a strong synergy amongst the products they produce. As pointed out in Chapter 1, Chinese society is much more interpersonal than Western societies, consumers care more about what their neighbors, friends and colleagues think. As a result, this approach is particularly effective in China.

Disadvantages: The market in China is still in its infancy. Segment-based market information is still quite thin. Currently, consumer-niche approaches can only be applied to broadly defined segments such as children, women and the elderly. Products targeted for more subtly defined segments require more in-depth knowledge and skills, and, for many companies, they risk missing those segments.

Value-niche approach

A company identifies an emerging demand for a product or service with a unique value added feature. The product or service may already exist in one form or another in the market place. The company offers the product with additional value added such as: easier access, lower price, more prestige, better packaging or better design. Increasingly, companies are adding atmosphere or "more pleasant access" to the purchase process. The experience of purchasing becomes as important as the product itself. One of the most successful examples of this are the Hard Rock Cafes in Beijing and Shanghai. These restaurants offer an environment redolent of the history of rock and roll music and have been profitable ever since they first opened.

Advantages: Consumers in China are becoming spoilt by the many purchasing options they are offered. The pressures of their working lives restrict their available time and direct them toward products or services which relieve time and efficiency concerns. They are also being drawn by other intangible qualities such as ambience and status. This is a signficant underlying trend in the market place and companies offering continuously upgraded value in their products and services should see sustained growth.

Disadvantages: This approach requires significant operational control over production quality, delivery and any other value added element. China's business infrastructure is still young and may not provide reliable means for offering value added features such as same day delivery across the country.

The approaches outlined above are generic options applied to the China market. Any company interested in entering — or expanding within — the market in China will have to employ broader based, better conceived and more concrete strategies to succeed.

The four options discussed may also serve companies already established in China. The market is constantly changing and developing and any company wishing to expand its operations will have to employ a sophisticated strategy of one kind or another to succeed. The product-niche approach might be the most relevant strategy for companies with products and services already in the field, but they may have to employ geo-niche, consumer-niche and value-niche strategies to supplement their core strategy if their goal is to reach more consumers, and penetrate the market more profoundly.

Companies entering the China market must realize how rich and varied the market is, particularly around the Pearl River Delta, Yangzi River Delta and in such major cities as Chengdu and Beijing. To enter such markets successfully, companies will have to provide products with values that differentiate them from the many other products available. In this case, product-niche and value-niche approaches apply. The other option of course is to identify an underdeveloped region offering little competition and employ a geo-niche strategy.

Stages of business development

In China, the potential is high, the market complex and the shifts fast. In this highly dynamic market, companies themselves are also moving extremely fast from market entry planning to operation establishment to rapid market development and eventually to business "saturation". No matter what stage a company is at in the process of pursuing the market opportunities in China, it faces a set of different yet specific challenges.

Business executives need to understand a large number of challenges and potential options for dealing with opportunities in China. Unfortunately a discussion about these issues in any detail is not within the scope of this book. Nevertheless some high level insights from a consumer and socio-cultural perspective are offered in the following section in the hope that business executives will gain a high level overview upon which further detailed and more comprehensive understanding can be built.

Planning stage

The planning stage is when a company starts to assess the market and business feasibility and to develop its approach and strategy before setting up any formal business operation in the market place.

There are a number of crucial questions to be answered during the planning period. What product is to be provided? What are the business potentials and risks involved? What approach and strategy is to be taken? Should a joint venture be developed? With whom should we build strategic partnerships? What is the critical level of commitment required?

To answer these questions, companies need to set their own foot physically into the relevant market place to understand the market. This means that the company not only needs to talk to potential business partners and stakeholders, but also, even more importantly in the context of this book, needs to talk to final purchasers and users at home and on the streets. The company not only needs to find out who the customers are, where they live, how they live, what they need, but also it needs to understand who are the purchasers, who are the final users, and what are the underlying social and cultural forces driving their consumption.

Figure 7.2 Business challenges at different stages

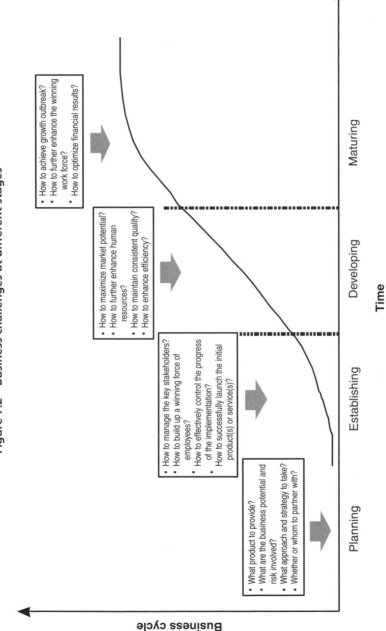

In China, the market potential is generally high and the environment extremely challenging. As a result, the responses from any third party to any feasibility questions are highly elastic and hence almost irrelevant. Many international and domestic industry and trade associations, general market and industry reports, governmental organizations (including embassies and consulates in the case of international companies) often provide valuable information and advice. Nevertheless, only through first-hand investigation, and by knowing its own capability, would a company be in the position of obtaining the relevant answers to its own questions. One of the important ingredients for getting a real answer is that business executives need to commit themselves to adapting to the ways of the culture, for example it may be appropriate to sit down and drink Maotai Liquor or Martell Cognac with local business connections.

Establishing stage

This is the stage when a company starts to set up its operation after a positive feasibility assessment. In this stage, a company often needs to obtain various licenses, set up offices and even manufacturing facilities, develop distribution channels and logistics and succeed in the initial market launch of its market entry product or service.

The company needs to know how to manage the expectations of the key stakeholders, including various business partners and governmental officials; how to successfully control the progress of the implementation; how to build up a winning force of employees; and how to successfully launch the initial product or service.

It is important to be aware of the fact that this stage should only be started after a critical commitment has been made for market entry or market expansion. The market in China is no longer a market that allows trials without critical commitment. Competition is fierce. Expectations are high. Trials without critical commitment often lead to negative results and jeopardize the entire entry effort.

It is also important for international business executives to leave their original value judgments at home before moving to China. Value perceptions and judgments are strongly underlined by culture. It seems to be a cliché yet an important reminder to stress that some behavior or value perceptions of the local people perceived as "wrong" by foreigners may make perfect sense to the local people in the local environment and vise versa. Doing business without drinking Maotai or Martell together means "heartless" to many local people. Presenting a gift which does not reflect the social status of the recipient means "mindless" or even "insulting". People in every region across China are extremely confident about their own culture and value. Do as the Romans do.

International business executives need to be aware of the fact that while many Western conceptual business frameworks are often great assets for succeeding in China, many Western approaches for implementing these frameworks would, however, only lead to disastrous results in the same market place. The notion, "it is not what you do, but how you do it," is probably more important in China than anywhere else. Adjusting and assimilating is one of the keys to carrying out successful business actions in China.

Developing stage

The developing stage represents a period in which a snowball effect for the business aspect, revenue in particular, of a company starts to happens. According to a 1996 consumer marketing survey by the Economist Intelligence Unit, 50% of the international consumer product manufacturers in China enjoyed a compounded annual growth rate of 30–100% for their revenue during the previous three years. And an additional 11% of the manufacturers had a compounded annual growth rate of 100–560% in the same period. Most of these companies were in the developing stage.

How does a company maximize market potential? How does it further enhance human resources? How does it maintain consistency in product quality? How does a company enhance effficiency? How does it balance revenue growth and profitability? To effectively address these issues, companies need to think ahead. Changes in the marketplace can be sudden. It is important to understand the sustainability of one's product or service towards certain relevant market trends. It is also important to understand the dimension and the structure of the relevant consumer base. As income levels rapidly rise, suitable geographic markets emerge and broaden at a high speed. In the meantime, the consumer base for additional products and services grows quickly.

To ensure longer-term market position, companies need to prepare for market expansion, considering customer segments, geographical coverage, business lines, distribution channels and value added features or services.

It is important for companies to make their own product obsolete before their competitors do. Markets in China develop fast. Domestic companies are quickly catching up with the latest technologies. International companies are shipping their latest products and services to the market place. Often the latest product or service innovations from some advanced countries reach the market place in China six months to one year earlier than they reach other advanced markets, particularly in the West. Companies need to upgrade their products in China's marketplace constantly and at a higher speed than they would in the West.

Maturing stage

Mr. Jack Welch, the CEO of GE from the US, pointed out that maturing business "is just a state of mind." However sooner or later, a company will start to face a set of different business challenges internally and externally. This generally happens when the growth of the focus market of a company starts to slowdown, when a company has already obtained commanding control in a focus market where it set out to dominate, or when some other event happens internally or externally.

How does a company achieve growth outbreak? The answer to this question shouldn't be difficult in present-day China, at least not yet. China has 1.2 billion people with a fast rising level of income. Its middle class population is obtaining a higher and higher level of income and its population is continuing to grow. China's market economy is still in its early stage. Vast consumer needs are still yet to be satisfied. Certainly there are forecasts that say by 2000 only 50% of the car manufacturing capacities in China will be able to find a market domestically. But most of the companies involved are playing longer term strategies and waiting for the market bang beyond 2000. If time proves, China's household rate for cars will, for a long period of time, not meet the expectations of the car manufacturers, and manufacturers will still have options to utilize or convert their capacities.

How to further enhance the winning work force? How to optimize the financial results? These questions need more thought.

While the right business questions need to be asked and many management approaches can be applied to answer them, the most important thing to remember is still what Mr. Welch pointed out that maturing business "is just a state of mind."

Keys to success

To succeed in China, companies need to do many things well. Of course each company has its own set of concerns specific to its sector or stage of business development in the market. Nevertheless, there are a number of specific critical factors to success in China's current consumer driven market place.

Have the most competent executive to be in charge of your China business

In its 26 May 1997 issue, *Business Week* pointed out, "No longer are China's 'special conditions' an excuse for tolerating years of losses. More often the problem is just a lousy business plan." It is useless to send anyone but your most competent executive to China to be in charge of your China business. The marketplace presents more challenges at a faster pace than any other environment your organization is working in. Competition is strong, culture is unique and unfamiliar, business mechanisms are different, consumers' tastes and demands shift rapidly, the regulatory environment changes constantly, the marketplace itself is complex and difficult to read. Further, business infrastructure is generally less developed, skilled professionals and laborers are difficult to keep, and the stakeholders in your business are often from many disciplines and backgrounds and can often exercise strong and unexpected powers.

All these challenges are still not everything. In China, no company can survive with a core-competence approach, the current management fad in the West. Every company simply needs to do everything necessary instead of only the "core" tasks to make their business work. To make a business work in China, business executives need to be multi-talented, at least now and for a considerable period of time still to come. No matter how large or small business operations may be, they need to play the role of a diplomat, a strategist, a manufacturing expert, and a distribution expert — all at the same time.

The simultaneous combination of these factors makes the marketplace in China one of the most challenging market environments in the world. Your operations will need to be guided by a strong, sure hand because otherwise the business will not develop smoothly or easily. Also your executive in China must have the complete support of the head office to succeed.

Identify and explore the underlying values and trends; avoid conclusions based on symptoms alone

It took Shanghai five years to realize a consumer market as mature as the one Taiwan achieved after 25 years. Everything in China moves fast. Strategists must learn to see past the typically dramatic symptoms of trends and aim for the underlying trend. The crest of the wave is a symptom, the trend is the wave itself. Companies must be proactively prepared for rapid change. They must constantly renew their products and services to suit the sustainable underlining trends.

McDonalds Restaurants is the best example to use here. The initial success of McDonalds in China comes from its novelty and entertainment value, not the taste or convenience of its food. I spoke to a number of domestic fast food operators and found that they are aiming to challenge McDonalds by providing a broad range of traditional foods with the modern convenience that is McDonalds greatest strength. For McDonalds to maintain growth it will have to address the more profound needs of the consumer.

Coca Cola is an icon of American culture. It has been exported to every corner of the globe successfully. However, within a decade after market entry into China, Coca Cola has already sensed the limitations of its carbonated drinks for the increasingly health conscious Chinese consumer. As a result, the company has brought out a line of natural juice based, non-carbonated drinks with a local joint-venture partner — a move that took Coca Cola almost a century in North America to make.

Many companies started their business successfully but failed to understand and keep up with the underlying trends of the consumer. For these companies, the symptoms of the trends change far too fast, and the market place is constantly evolving in an unknown direction. They are confused with the schizophrenia of the marketplace and its underlying trends. As a result, a large portion have seen their business decline or even disappear in China.

Provide real and unique value

As in the West, the value of consumer goods in China falls into four categories: utilitarian, convenience, social and emotional. Chapter 5 showed how Chinese consumers are becoming increasingly sensitive to intangible values. It also illustrated why Chinese consumers are prepared to pay more for the social value of goods and services than consumers in the West.

Bristol Myers Squib has been very successful selling vitamins in China in spite of the fact that China is the largest vitamin manufacturer in the world. The key to their success is the special value added feature of the galenic formulation of the vitamin. The vitamins, like many other medicines in pill or capsule format, are encased in a covering or coating formulated to assist in the absorption of the medication's chemical component. The percentage of any pill or capsule containing the medicinal ingredient is small, the majority of the pill or capsule is composed of a filler and coating designed to assist the body's natural digestive process. China is still behind the rest of the world in its galenic technology.

In 1995, China produced a list of pharmaceuticals that the government would be willing to pay for in the event of illness. It's an idea similar to the approved list of drugs insurance policies might cover. The list held 1,400 branded drugs. In China, there are 20,000–30,000 drugs on the market. No serious medication will succeed unless it reaches the approved list. The criteria for acceptance on the list is related to the specific values of the product. Only those drugs with specific value added features such as high reputation, enhanced efficacy, and favorable price make it onto the list.

Although the market economy in China is still less than 20 years old, it is a big mistake to consider the marketplace as one that is underdeveloped. Business professionals need to remember that many of the world's latest product or service innovations are now appearing in the China market a half year earlier than in the West. The market in China often offers larger selections than the market in the West. For example, residents in Shanghai enjoy at least 700 different vegetables, Beijing residents enjoy a selection of over 110 different brands of skin care products, and people from across the country enjoy a selection of almost all of the conceivable brands of beer available on the planet. If we say the telephone household rate in China's urban areas is still lower than that in the West, then the video CD (VCD) player household rate in China's urban areas will be considerably higher than that in the West. A senior executive of the well known American warehouse retailer Wal-Mart told me that he and his colleagues were surprised to discover that the best selling items were large screen TV sets when they opened up their first warehouse retail shop in China. But should they be surprised?

Adopt Chinese values

In Chapter 1, the assimilating nature of Chinese society was discussed, how it draws everything into itself, consumes it, then transforms it into something organically Chinese. The consumption behaviors of Chinese consumers are far more determined by their own purchasing power, their own social and cultural background and their own life patterns than any influences from outside.

For example, the American-style washing machine (with vertical spinning mechanism) introduced by Japanese companies in the 1980s used to dominate the China market. However only some ten years later, the favor of the Chinese consumers has already turned to the European style washing machines (with horizontal rolling tunnel mechanism), as they believe that this kind of washing machine is better suited to their ever upgrading quality of clothes, because this mechanism saves the fiber from severe twisting during the washing process. The trend remains the same, but the symptom has changed.

The Japanese manufacturers dominate the color television market in almost every country around the world. However in less than 20 years after the introduction of color TVs from Japan into China, the market is now dominated by Chinese domestic brands.

Business professionals need to realize that Chinese consumers follow the natural course of their development instead of any outside influence that does not suit their needs. In the course of this development, they will pick up only the things that are suitable to them for one reason or another.

Due to ongoing socio-economic transformation in China, the country and its people are rapidly evolving from within. Strategists must watch and understand the whole society, and continually adapt their products and services to the evolving needs of that society. They must make their products and services an integrated element of the society. They can retain their "foreign-ness", but they must also fit harmoniously into the Chinese value system.

Perhaps the soundest advice is to leave any and all preconceptions about your products and services and their potential benefits to the Chinese consumer, at home. You enter another world in China, different rules and different expectations, where the brightest mind is the most open mind.

Challenges ahead

China's present economy is new and without comparison in the rest of the world. It is an economy still sorting itself out and still struggling to define itself. But there are certain key issues that make this new economy particularly challenging for Western businesses accustomed to functioning in more mature economies.

Short product cycle

First, and most importantly, China's economy is in a state of flux and constant evolution, and it is changing at a greater speed than any other economy in the world. Incomes are rising, infrastructure improving, competition increasing, and more and more international businesses are jumping in to stir the pot. The golden rule seems to be that what happens over decades somewhere else, happens in China in only a few years, or months. Products have short life cycles, new ideas are consumed, digested and replaced almost overnight. Most importantly, China's consumers have the shortest attention span and the least patience. They know what they want and they want it now.

Presently, business ideas, products and investment are flowing into China, but it won't be long before China becomes an exporter, not only of products and services but also of ideas. China's best business minds have been idle for decades. The energy and atmosphere of the new economy will stimulate ideas as well as increase GDP. China has four times the population of the United States. Imagine the consequences when China begins producing as many brilliant inventions and innovations per capita as the United States has produced in the past few years. The impact would be staggering if China only developed half as many new ideas per capita as the United States.

Of course, this is about China developing the natural resource of its own people, but it also underlines how important it is for international business to be present in China when these innovations begin. Western nations made a strategic business error by ignoring Japan's early business innovations. Many only woke up after Japan had taken a considerable chunk of market share. Energy feeds on energy, and ideas spawn ever more ideas. By 2010, according to the current trends, China will be well on its way to becoming a leading world economy.

The rapid spread of economic development throughout China

The early development of the economy can be tracked easily. It began in the Pearl River Delta in the late 1970s, moved to the Jiaodong and Liaodong Peninsulas in the 1980s, and to the Yangzi River Delta in the 1990s. Now, it is spreading to the Bohai Bay region and the resource-rich regions inland. China's consumers encourage economic development with their voracious consumer appetites.

How does a foreign business enter this new world? Where, when and how? It is increasingly difficult to make these decisions as the playing field is forever changing. Fierce competition makes risk-taking dangerous.

In the early days it was much easier for international companies to target their point of entry. The infrastructure system was not very well developed and transportation routes were rudimentary. Any significant cargo being shipped a long distance would have to go by rail. Today, highways are spreading across the country, and consumer centers are no longer clustered just around the Pearl River Delta, the Yangzi River Delta or the Bohai Bay region. Certainly, these highly developed centers are important hubs for distribution, but there are newer regions inland and developments along the entire coast which are becoming important consumer markets.

Significant regional differences

There is no one quality that defines the China market, because it is a market made up of many different regions, with many different characteristics. In terms of regional market breakdown, there are the Pearl River and Yangzi River Deltas, the Beijing/Bohai Bay market, the Jiaodong Peninsula market, the Liaodong Peninsula market, the Greater Wuhan market, the Chongqing-Chengdu market, among many others. New markets and regions will continue to develop if only because of China's extraordinary size and diversity. The east-west land span of China is over 5,000 km, and its north-south land span over 3,500 km. China is made up of 27 provinces plus four provincial level cities and 55 nationalities.

Perhaps the easiest way to define each region is by its customs, eating habits and food. In the provinces of Zhejiang and Jiangsu they prefer food that is delicate, natural in color and lightly salted.

In Sichuan, they prefer spicy food and mix hot chilli peppers with everything, rendering most food red. In my home town of Beijing, they flavor their food with black bean sauce or soya sauce until it's almost black. In Shanghai, it's customary for the man to pick up the bill, but in Hangzhou, barely 300 km away, it's not uncommon for the woman to pay the bill. The average per capita income of Beijing residents is 7% lower than Shanghai residents, but Beijing's residents, on average, are more generous with beggars in the street. A 1994 survey by Zero Point Market Survey and Analysis Ltd, Beijing, showed that people in Shanghai donate an average of RMB 0.21 each time to beggars in the streets, which is only 60% as much as the average amount which is donated by the people in Beijing. Curiously, and as an observation, the average per capita income of residents in Shanghai is over 10% higher than that of Beijing's generous residents. In Beijing, more money is spent on skin cream per capita than in

Figure 7.3   Income growth by region, 1986–90

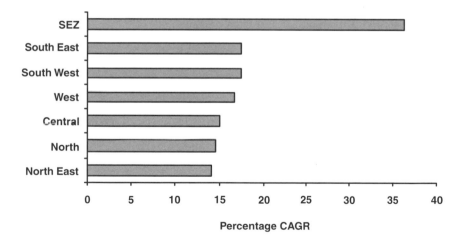

Percentage CAGR

Note: SEZ refers to special economic zones
Source: Setting Up Shop, Retailing in China, 1996, reproduced by permission of FT Pitman Publishing

Shanghai because of the drier climate. Young women in Chengdu wear the most scandalous current fashions. The people of the province of Xinjiang are known for their generosity, their capacity for spending, and their joy of life. In Xinjiang, women enjoy drinking large amounts of hard liquor, which is generally a pastime for men in most other parts of China. Of course, these are generalizations, and perhaps clichés, but it serves to point out the complexity and breadth of this market.

Figure 7.4   Urban residents income and living expenditure, 1995

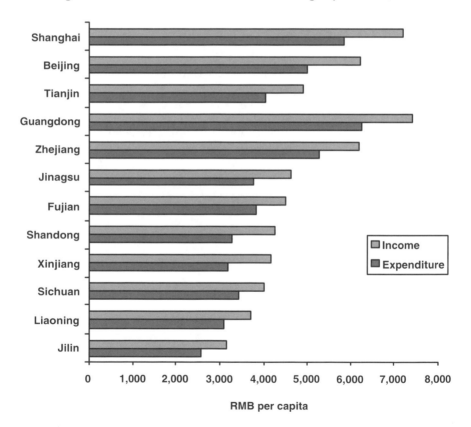

Data compiled from: China Statistical Yearbook, 1996

Each region has its own specific needs due to climate, location and income level. For example, in Shangdong province there is a large market for frozen food in part because of the high ownership rate of refrigerators and freezers.

The market for personal care products in Beijing is dominated by skin creams because the air is dry and cold in winter, and extremely hot in summer. In Shanghai, the weather is milder and more money is spent on hair care products.

Figure 7.5   Urban ownership of household appliances, 1995

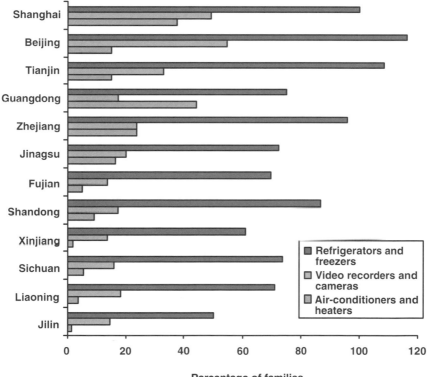

Percentage of families

Data compiled from: China Statistical Yearbook, 1996

Figure 7.6   Market share of personal care products in Beijing, 1995

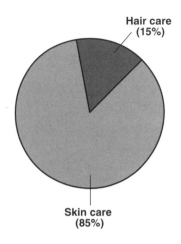

Data compiled from: National Information Center, analysis of Deloitte Consulting, 1996

Figure 7.7   Market share of personal care products in Shanghai, 1995

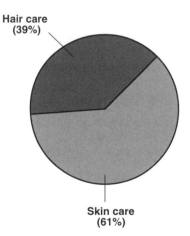

Data compiled from: National Information Center, analysis of Deloitte Consulting, 1996

Rapid polarization of consumer purchasing power

There are serious issues that threaten business activities. The gap between rich and poor is growing. In the past in urban centers, there were few who lived below the Chinese Survival Limit (CSL), the level at which life is sustainable and the level which was estimated at RMB 1,130 p.a. by the State Statistical Bureau of China in 1994. According to State statistics, the number of urban people living below the CSL reached 12–15 million, or 5% of all urban residents. This number has increased and continues to grow because of jobs lost in the process of industry restructuring and economic transformation.

By 1995, 44% of State-owned enterprises in China were losing money. At the end of 1996, losses by State-owned enterprises reached RMB 60.3 billion, a jump of 47% over the previous year.

The realities of the market economy will eventually force State enterprises to adjust or shut down. To adjust to the new sink or swim environment, China adopted its first bankruptcy law in 1986. Unfortunately, total bankruptcies have increased annually since 1990.

Figure 7.8   Annual number of bankrupt companies in China

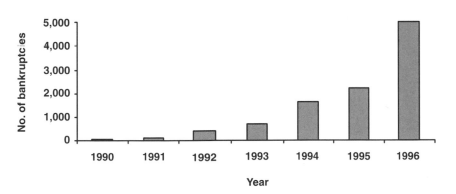

Data compiled from: *Information Express*, Guangzhou, 1997

Between 1994 and 1995, the working population of Shanghai declined by 87,000 to 4.77 million. This is a result of business failures, lay-offs and increasing automation. Automation has had a particularly forceful impact on Shanghai's renowned textile industry.

At least 47 million young people will be entering the labor force between 1995 and 2000. Of the 47 million, 40 million will find work replacing retiring employees, or in new jobs, but seven million will remain unemployed.

The elderly between 65 and 75 have the lowest average income of any group surveyed. Those living on pensions have difficulty making ends meet and are quietly slipping toward the CSL.

In 1994, the poorest 20% of China's total households took in only 4.27% of the total national private household income, while the richest 20% of households accrued a stunning 50.24% of the same total. This rich-poor polarization is already significantly wider than that of the US and is still growing.

In 1996, a survey of 35 major cities showed that 40% of all urban families saw their per capita income decline from the year before. This occurred in spite of the fact that the overall per capita income of urban residents grew net of inflation 3.4% from 1995 to 1996.

As the income gap widens, the income distribution curve of Chinese consumers begins to flatten. The markets for high-priced consumer items and low-priced consumer goods begins to polarize. The middle income or mid-range consumer will continue to be the most important consumer segment. But this segment's dominance of the market will decline as the high end and lower end market segments begin to exert further influence. As a result, market entry will depend on targeting specific consumer segments or niches. It is not enough anymore to throw the dice and hope for the best.

Figure 7.9   Comparison of income distribution past vs future

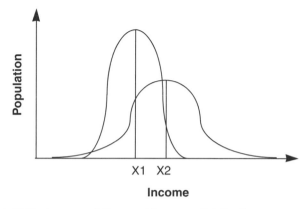

Note: X1 — statistical mean of the past income distribution
        X2 — statistical mean of the future income distribution

Impact of RMB appreciation

The RMB is significantly undervalued. In 1997, the official exchange rate was about US$1 = RMB 8.3, however based on World Bank estimates, the actual purchasing power parity of the currencies is US$1 << RM 2. The purchasing power of RMB is over four times as high as what official exchange rates suggest. The Chinese Government has purposefully kept the exchange rate low in order to boost its exports. The Central Bank of China has been buying great quantities of US dollars with the RMB to keep the RMB from appreciating against the dollar. By March 1997, China's foreign reserves had surpassed US$114 billion, the second largest foreign reserves held by any country in the world.

Obviously, the government won't hold the RMB back forever. When the RMB begins to appreciate, the purchasing power of Chinese consumers will increase significantly. The RMB will not be appreciated to as high as the equivalent rate suggested by the

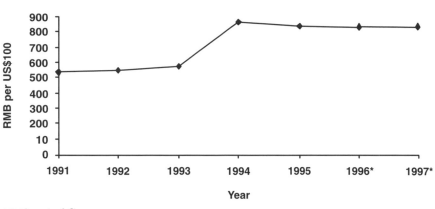

Figure 7.10   Exchange rate RMB vs US$

*Estimated figure
Data compiled from: China Statistical Yearbook, Deloitte Consulting, 1997

purchasing power parity; however, appreciation of the RMB is inevitable.

The appreciation of the RMB will offer new opportunities for international businesses. Many products that are now only viable because of local manufacture will be imported. Many international manufacturers, who have not seen a place for their products in China's market will enter the market as exporters to China.

Domestic and international companies already in the market place need to prepare carefully for the inevitable economic changes that will follow RMB appreciation, as this will lead to an even more competitive and complex environment. In the future, China's market will shift from a two-sided competitive base, or competition between domestic companies and companies from advanced economies, to a three-sided competitive base, or competition between domestic competitors, competitors from advanced economies, and competitors from less developed economies such as Vietnam, Pakistan and India. This process has already begun. During one of my trips to Urumqi, I was looking for an Urgur jacket as a souvenir for my wife and

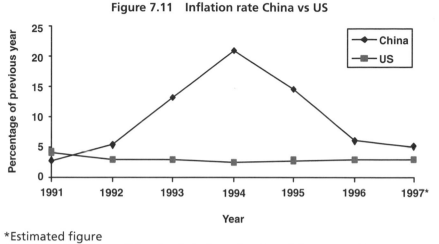

Figure 7.11   Inflation rate China vs US

*Estimated figure
Data compiled from: China Statistical Yearbook, Deloitte Consulting, 1997

found that all the Urgur jackets and hats available at private- or State-owned stores had been manufactured in Pakistan.

Staying on top

China is now in its best shape ever. Its economy has every reason to continue to grow quickly. Its consumer market has every reason to continue to boom.

Before 1997, economists and strategists around the world were waiting, although unwillingly, for the passing of Deng Xiaoping, and were concerned about who would succeed him. With Deng's death, the succession has been smooth. The new leaders continue to further reform China's economic system and to further open up its economy and market to the world.

As of 1 July 1997, Hong Kong successfully transferred back to China after more than 150 years of British rule. As a regional economic power, Hong Kong is expected to have a significant impact on many aspects of China. While the world expects China to have a strong impact on Hong Kong's future social, political and economic development, it also expects Hong Kong to have at least an equivalent impact on the future development of China. The leaders of China have been asking and will continue to ask what makes this small region so economically powerful? Answers to this question will lead to actions that will greatly strengthen the continued economic success of China. With further socio-economic integration between Hong Kong and China, it is inevitable that Hong Kong's capital, management expertise, product innovations, consumption pattern and entrepreneurial spirit will be transferred to mainland China in greater depth and scale.

If Hong Kong will add to the socio-economic development in China significantly, the planned return of the Portuguese colony Macao will add to this process, too. Macao will return to China in 1999. Although Macao's socio-economic power and influence in the region is not comparable to Hong Kong's, it will nevertheless be another building block in the development of China's increasingly market-oriented economy and consumer society.

Although Taiwan and mainland China are still at odds politically, their economic ties are already very strong. One of the largest portions of overseas investment in mainland China comes from Taiwan. Business people from Taiwan have set up countless business operations across mainland China, from Shenzhen to Beijing and from Harbin to Urumqi. They manufacture and provide a wide range of products and services from footwear to computers and from wedding photo studios to theme parks. In early 1997 the first direct commercial seafreight cargo route between mainland China and Taiwan opened. Further economic interaction will add to the momentum of the economic development in mainland China.

Business infrastructure and environment in China is improving rapidly. Telecommunications has reached almost every corner of the country. Electricity has reached over 90% of households. Many regions which used to be isolated from the rest of the country due to the lack of roads are now connected not only with roads but often highways. New expressways, new railways and new airports are continuously appearing on the map of the country. Although the legal system is still behind its economic development, China is now much more sophisticated than at the beginning of the 1980s and it is developing rapidly. The price and pricing systems for goods and services have been successfully transformed from planned to market-driven systems. Credit cards, debit cards and personal cheques have become popular in almost all regions. Local businesses are now more familiar and skilled with market economy and international trade than ever before. Economic reform is happening everywhere. The economic development has now started to move inland and towards agriculture, which further enhances the sustainability of the economic development of the past 19 years. The educational level of the Chinese people, particularly given market-oriented knowledge education and skill training, is rapidly advancing. Consumers, although some more than others, are now more in tune with international products, services, consumption tastes and patterns than ever before.

I left China in the early 1980s to pursue my career in the West. At that time, it never occurred to me that any of my future professional activities would involve China or business in China. But times have changed and many of us who left China to study and to work abroad find ourselves applying all the experiences and expertise we have gained in the West to the challenges of China's economic boom and consumer revolution.

Certainly, China still faces daunting challenges including significant regional disparities, swelling bankruptcies, climbing unemployment, growing polarization between the rich and the poor, spreading drug consumption, AIDS and crime. The western media feeds off these issues and often ends up dismissing the significant market opportunities and the available effective business options. But the developments are real, the successes substantial, and the international business community is convinced that opportunities far outweigh risks.

China's economy has been developing with great vigor, and now it has every reason to develop with even greater vigor than ever before.

China is set to dominate the world's economy.

Glossary

ambience Refers to the qualities of an object or activity that are aesthetically, spiritually, or emotionally pleasing, such as the design of a certain good or the atmosphere of a restaurant.

assimilation Refers to the nature of Chinese society, how it draws everything into itself, consumes it, then transforms it into something organically Chinese.

ATM Automatic transaction machine. Generally called bank cash machine.

CAGR Compounded annual growth rate. Often expressed in percent and used to describe the speed of the growth of certain measurable phenomena, such as growth of economy or revenue.

consumer Refers to both the end user and the purchaser of goods or services.

Development Zones Refers to regions or zones (over 360) across China where international and local enterprises receive advantageous treatment particularly in tax rates. This term includes the often referred to Five Special Economic Zones in China.

expressway Refers to the recently developed, enclosed roads which allow high speed traffic up to 130 km per hour.

fangbianmian Chinese name for instant noddle.

FDI Foreign direct investment. In 1996, China utilized US$42.4

billion in FDI and was one of the world's largest nations in FDI utilization.

GDP Gross domestic product. By the end of 1996, China's GDP had already surpassed US$4 trillion based on purchasing power parity.

GSM Global system of mobile communication. A kind of digital cellular network with wide coverage.

highway Cross regional roads mainly designed for motor vehicles.

Hukou A registration system which registers the residency of all people in China and was used to control the permanent cross regional movements of all Chinese citizens. The Hukou system controlled people's movement by refusing them the social benefits which are often essential for living and only entitled to the residents officially registered in the area under consideration.

Hutong A modest laneway consisting of masonry walls punctuated with doors leading to low rise accommodation around a shared courtyard. This is the traditional construction of residential areas in China.

interpersonal Refers to the strong tendency of the individual to relate to other people or other people's opinions. In China, the individual's identity is always determined by how others view him or her.

life extension Describes the desire for a long life and reverence for the elderly and children in the Chinese culture. It is not only about extending one's own life, it also means a deeply felt connection to ancestors and future generations. It is as if the individual is standing in the middle of an empty field holding onto a long rope suspended at waist level. The rope represents all past and future generations.

OTC Over the counter pharmaceutical product. Officially there are no OTC pharmaceutical products yet, but China is expected to legalize this category before 2000.

PPP Purchasing power parity. Designed to compare the purchasing power of different currencies distorted by the pure exchange rate. It is often used to assess the economic strength of certain regions or countries more realistically.

purchaser Refers to the buyer because of the significant disconnection between the people who will use certain goods or services and the people who buy them.

Qigong Ancient Chinese exercise which, it is believed, streamlines the inner energy flow of the human body and mind, vitalizes the human body and the mind, even cures diseases.

Qijing Refers to Nature's beauty at its utmost. The Qijings across the country have attracted Chinese poets and scholars for over 2000 years.

RMB The currency of the People's Republic of China. Its currency exchange rate against US$1 has been around RMB 8.28 to RMB 8.32 with a slide trend of appreciation.

s-generation Refers to the first generation born shortly before and after the official installation of China's single child policy in 1978.

ss-generation Refers to the single children of the s-generation. The ss-generation will, together with the s-generation, build two very significant generations in China's future history.

three-dimensional living Refers to the change of the Chinese people's life from a "work unit-home" linear pattern to a "work unit-anywhere out of the home-home" triangular pattern. The "anywhere out of the home" portion is demanding increasingly more time and higher financial resources.

Xiahai A verb meaning "plunge into the sea". It is a common term used to describe those that had plunged into the market economy from State-owned organizations and enterprises in China.

Xiao Xian Fu Chinese term for leisure clothes, the clothes of less rigid design, supple and comfortable to wear.

References

— 1994, Almanac of China's Population, Economic Management Publishing House, Beijing, China.

— 1995, 'Forster's Brews a China Strategy', Crossborder Monitor, 18 Oct.

— 1996, 'Asian at Play - A Good Day Out', *The Economist*, 21 Dec.

— 1996, 'Asians At Play', *The Economist*, 21 Dec.

— 1996, 'Beijingers Envy Wealthy, Powerful: Opinion Study on Beijing Residents by Beijing Television Station and Capital Normal University's Political and Law Department', *South China Morning Post*, 5 Oct.

— 1996, 'Cash Culture Sweeps Aside Political Issues', *South China Morning Post*, 5 Oct.

— 1996, 'China – Business Report', The Economic Intelligent Unit, 2nd Quarter.

— 1996, 'China, The Money and the Muck', *The Economist*, 16 Nov.

— 1996, 'Choose Focus, Develop Fishery', *Information Express*, 16 Oct.

— 1996, 'Little Emperors Call the Shots', *Asia Business*, Sept.

— 1996, 'No Wall's Too High', *Business China*, 5 Feb.

— 1996, 'The Red Capitalist Rong Zhijian', *Cai Fu*, No. 8, Oct.

— 1996, 'The Right Formula', *Business China*, 19 Feb.

— 1996, 'With Footprint All Over the Country', *Information Express*, 16 Oct.

— 1996, Fine Shopping Guide Weekly, Beijing, China, July.

— 1997, '20 Biggest Populations, 2050 Forecast', *The Economist*, 1 Feb.

— 1997, 'Both Feet in the Door - Mary Kay's Direct Marketing', *Business China*, 14 April.

— 1997, 'Can China Deliver the Goods?', *The Economist*, 15 Feb.

— 1997, 'China on the Move', *The Economist*, 8 Feb.

— 1997, 'Deng is Dead - So What? Economic Stewardship Is Not A Question. Political Leadership Is', *Business China*, 24 Feb.

— 1997, 'Emerging-Market Indicators', *The Economist*, 7 June.

— 1997, 'How Hong Kong Can Change China', *The Economist*, 28 June.

— 1997, 'Lucky Larry - CITIC Pacific', *The Economist*, 4 Jan.

— 1997, 'On Drugs - Despite an industry-wide slump, China's pharmaceutical market continues to wow foreign investors with its potential', *Business China*, 6 Jan.

— 1997, 'Set Fair - For the Chinese Economy, 1997 Will Be a Good Year. It Should Prove an Even Better Year for Foreign Investors', *Business China*, 20 Jan.

Abramson, Neil R. & Ai, Janet X. 1995, 'Taking the Slow Boat to China?', *Business Quarterly*, 59(3), pp. 29-37.

Abramson, R. Neil & Ai, Janet X. 1996, 'You Get What You Expect In China', *Business Quarterly*, 61(2), pp. 37-44.

Ayala, J., Lai, R., Mok, B., Wei, F. & Zhang, H. 1996, 'Winning China's Consumer Market in the 21st Century', *The McKinsey Quarterly*, No. 2, pp. 178-92.

Barret, Christophe & Slaughter, Andrew 1995, 'Whither Chinese Energy Policy?', *Electric Perspectives*, July-Aug.

Bernstein, Richard & Munro, Ross H. 1997, 'China I: The Coming Conflict with America', *Foreign Affairs*, 76(2), pp. 18-32.

Buczek, Mark 1996, 'Fueling China's Growth', *The China Business Review*, Oct.

Cha, Guan 1996, 'Incredible PC Potential Triggers Cutthroat Competition', *Business Beijing*, May-June.

Chan, Anita & Senser, Robert A. 1997, 'China's Troubled Workers', *Foreign Affairs*, 76(2), pp. 104-17.

Chin, David & Towler, William 1995, 'Retail: Opportunities and Obstacles', *Institutional Investor*, Nov.

De Keijzer, Arne J. 1995, China, Business Strategies for the '90s, *Pacific View Press*, Berkeley, California.

Enright, Michael J., Scott, Edith E. & Dodwell, David 1997, *The Hong Kong Advantage*, Oxford University Press, New York.

Fangyu, Lui & Shaolong, Zhang 1994, 'Analysis of Consumption Structure of the Chinese Consumer in the Late 90s', Journal of Beijing University, 2, 14-48. Fengxi, Zhang 1996, 'Personal Cheques Coming of Age', *Economic Life Weekly*, 26 Sept.

Gelb, Catherine 1996, 'Anyone's Guess', *The China Business Review*, May-June.

Gold, Thomas 1991, 'Can Pudong Deliver?', *The China Business Review*, Nov-Dec.

Grant, Linda 1997, 'GE's "Smart Bomb" Strategy', *Fortune*, 21 July.

Hamer, Andrew Marshall 1995, 'Cashing In On China's Burgeoning Middle Class', *Marketing Management*, 4(1), Summer.

Janguang, Tan 1996, 'The Role Change of the Farmers in the Pearl River Delta', *Sociology Research*, 65, pp. 81-6.

Keqiang, Yang & Ke, Oyang 1995, 'Analysis of the Current Consumer of China', *Journal of Si Chuan University*, 1, pp. 17-21.

Lardy, R. Nicholas 1996, 'The PRC Economy Appears Stable for Now, Despite Lurking Problems', *The China Business Review*, May-June.

Lenzner, Robert 1995, 'Buy China - Carefully', *Forbes*, 13 Mar.

Li, Dong & Gallup, Alec M. 1996, 'In Search of the Chinese Consumer', *The China Business Review*, Sept-Oct.

Li, Shaomin, Gao, Yuxian & Ma, Guangqin, 'Picking the Winners in Profitability and Productivity', *The China Business Review*, July-Aug.

Li, Xiao 1996, 'Largest City Group Attracts Global Attention', *Information Weekly*, 14 June.

Ligong, Li 1996, 'Radio TV Stations Develop Fast', *China Daily*, 31 Oct.

Lyle, Gwen 1996, 'Consumer Goods and Retail in the PRC: Getting US Goods on the Shelves', *Business America*, Jan.

Ministry of Agriculture Various years, China Agriculture Almanac, China Agriculture Publishing House, Beijing, China.

Ministry of International Trade 1993, Investment Guide of China, Zhong Xin Publishing House, People's Republic of China.

Norman, James R. 1994, 'A Very Nimble Elephant', *Forbes*, 10 Oct.

Patten, Chris 1997, 'Beyond the Myths', *The Economist*, 4 Jan.

Pawlyna, Andrea 1996, 'Packed to Perfection', *Asia Business*, Mar.

Peng, Foo Choy 1996, 'Youngster Opt For Lucrative Career At Home', *South China Morning Post Information Weekly*, 28 Dec.

Pollay, Richard, W., Tse, David & Wang, Zheng-Yuan 1990, 'Advertising, Propaganda and Value Change in Economic Development –

The New Cultural Revolution in China and Attitudes Towards Advertising', *Journal of Business Research*, 20(2), pp. 83-96.

Qinglian, He 1996, 'Analysis of the Current Rich and Poor Polarization', *Book Extracts Magazine*, Feb.

Ross, Robert S. 1997, 'China II: Beijing as a Conservative Power', *Foreign Affairs*, 76(2), pp. 33-44.

Scarry, Joseph 1996, 'Putting Children First', *The China Business Review*, May-June.

Simbek, Dale R., Dickenson, Ronald L. & Carter, L.D. 1994, 'China's Coal Use', *Independent Energy*, July-Aug.

Spence, Jonathan & Chin, Annping 1997, 'Deng's Heirs', *The New Yorker*, Beijing, 10 March.

Spence, Jonathan & Zeng, Nian 1997, 'A Flood of Troubles', *The New York Times Magazine*, 5 Jan.

Swanson, Mitzi 1995, 'China Puts on a New Face', *The China Business Review*, Sept-Oct.

Tanzer, Andrew 1996, 'The Pacific Century', *Forbes*, 15 July.

Tanzer, Andrew 1997, 'Stepping Stones to a New China?', *Forbes*, 27 Jan.

Tong, Qian & Jia, Chen 1996, 'BDA – Potential Growth Point of Economy', *Business Beijing*, Sept.

Tse, David 1994, 'Cultural Differences in Conducting Intra- and Inter-Cultural Negotiations: A Sino-Canadian Comparison', *Journal of International Business Studies*, pp. 537-55.

Tse, David, Belk, Russell W. & Zhou, Nan 1989, 'Becoming a Consumer Society: A Longitudinal and Cross-Cultural Content Analysis of Print Ads from Hong Kong, the People's Republic of China, and Taiwan', *Journal of Consumer Research*, March, pp. 457-72.

Vanhonaker, Wilfried 1997, 'Entering China: An Unconventional Approach', *Harvard Business Review*, 75(2), pp. 130-40.

—Various years, China Light Industry Yearbook, Yearbook House of China Light Industry, Light Industry Association, Beijing, China.

Warner, Fara 1997, 'Foreign Brands Don't Impress Chinese Consumers', *The Asia Wall Street Journal*, 24 Mar.

Weixiong, Zhang 1995, 'Low Price Housing Have the Highest Demand', *Information Weekly*, 28 July.

Wong, Lana 1997, 'Cultural Values Crucial to Selling in Mainland Market', *South China Morning Post*, 22 Feb.

Xiangqiao, Zhang & Minwen, Hong 1993, Sociology of ResidentialHousing, Publishing House for Social Science Papers, Beijing, China.

Yujin, Gu 1995, "Adults Are Forced to Use Infant Skin Care Products', *Information Weekly*, 28 July.

Zhang, Yong & Gelb, Betsy D. 1996, 'Matching Advertising Appeals to Culture: The Influence of Products', *Journal of Advertising*, XXV(3), Fall, pp. 29-46.

Zhijian, Huang 1994, 'The Life Style and its Trends of the Contemporary Young Generation', *Liao Wang Magazine*.

Zhiqiang, Qiao & Ping, Zhang 1994, 'Analysis of Consumption Level and Structure of Rural Residents in Huabei', *Journal of Shanxi University*, pp. 25-30.

Index

24 hour shops 102
60+ consumers 13, 33, 34 50-1, 69-76, 181

Acer Peripherals Suzhou Co. Ltd. 84
agriculture 45, 76
AIDS 7, 224
air passenger freight capacity 43
airline industry 23, 136
airports 223
Alcatel 39
ambience 123-31
An Ju Le Ye 160
Anju housing 164
appliances (see electrical appliances)
Asian Wall Street Journal 19, 161
assimilation 7, 17-20, 225
AT&T 39

Ba Xian Zhuo 14
baby boomers 50
Bang & Olufsen 27
bank deposits 172, 176
Bank of China 40, 41
banking and investment services 179
banking, electronic 175
bankrupt companies 217
bars and cafes 32, 107, 125, 128
beauty salons 124
Beijing Economic and Technological Development Area (BDA) 85
Beijing-Kowloon Railway 111

Beijing-Tianjin-Tangshan Delta 88
Beitaipingzhuang Food Supermarket 102
Bose 27
bottled water 147
boutiques 25
Bristol Myers Squib 207
Buddhism 153
business infrastructure 7
Business Week 205

CAIFU (Wealth) 2, 24
cars 135, 161
    luxury 25
    manufacturers 81, 87, 204
CD players 208
Central Bank of China 219
cheques 41
chicken processing 93
Child's Life Long Happiness insurance 180
China National Petroleum Corporation 97
China Scholarship Council 185
China-Singapore Suzhou Industrial Park 78-9
Chinese Bank of Industry and Commerce 41
Chinese Survival Limit 217-18
Chongqing 84-5
cigarettes 18
cities 59, 63, 66-8 , 72, 89
CNN 36
coal 95-7
coastal regions 47
Coca Cola 20, 147, 207
coffee 32

Confucius 15
Construction Bank of China 41
consumers 18, 27, 35, 50, 122, 160
    centers 78-80
    market 206
    price level 23
    revolution 13-20
consumer-niche approach 196
contract employment 110
Conversation Stations 71
credit card system 40
crime 7, 224
Cultural Revolution 4, 33, 76, 100-1, 131
currency trading 176

Daoism 153
Deng Xiaoping 2, 4, 120, 122, 221
deposit rates 179
Development Zones 29, 31, 47, 68, 85, 225
dairy products 32
DINKS 189
drugs 208, 224

Economic Daily, 141
economic reforms 50
Economist Intelligence Unit 3, 202
education 16, 59, 73-5, 103, 155
education and telecommunications 183- 9
edutainment 108
eel processing 93
efficiency 131-43
electrical appliances 19, 93, 161

electricity 15, 95-6, 154, 223
enterprises, collective 66
entertainment 101, 103, 126
entrepreneurs 23, 92, 122

families 9, 35, 72, 123
famine 4
fangbianmian 134, 225
farmers 6-7, 59-60, 62-6, 90, 111-12, 139, 155, 157
fiber optic cables 85
fishing industry 67
Five Year Plan,
    Eighth (1991-1995) 21
    Ninth (1996-2000) 21, 68, 81, 94-5, 115, 164
flower shops 125
food 144, 212-13

foreign direct investment (FDI) 21, 225
    investment 29
    reserves 21
freight capacity 42

gas, natural 95-7
GDP 2, 21, 66, 100, 226
geo-niche approach 195-6
gifts 14
Global System of Mobile Communication (GSM) 39, 226
Goh Chok Tong 7
government 43-7, 64, 68, 84, 87, 92, 94-5
    bonds 176
policy 162
Great Wall Card 40

Great Wall Hotel 193
Guanxi 2-3, 13-4

Hard Rock Cafe 197
health 116, 143-52
   and fitness clubs 152
   and lifestyle 148
   care 179
   care reform 162
   foods 145
   black 146
   green 145
   red 147
   tonics 13
highrise commercial/residential construction 167
home improvement 160-71
   ownership 161
Hong Kong 221-2
hotels 27, 31, 112-13
household furniture 161
housing industry 161
   traditional 80
Hukou system 5, 13, 43, 69, 109-10, 114-15, 124-6, 130, 226

income 23-7, 39, 45, 64-5
individuals 14, 153
infrastructure 36-43, 40, 66
inheritance 9, 10
insurance industry 179-82
interaction 20
interior decoration 170
International Herald Tribune 37

international trade 21, 212
Internet 39, 40, 57, 131-2, 138
Internet Cafe 9 40
interpersonal 7, 11-15, 226
infrastructures 212
investment and insurance 171-83
investors 88, 94

Jialing Industrial Company 84
Jianguo Hotel 193
Jie Gui 29
Jingcai (see vegetables)
Jingjishiyong housing 164

Ke Ju system 15
Khan, Genghis 18
knowledge 15-16, 51, 154

Lee Kuan Yew 78
Legal Daily 62
libraries 108
life expectancy 70
life extension 7, 9-11, 226
life insurance 172
    joint venture 183
little emperors 6
living space 26, 123

magazines (see newspapers)
Mary Kay Corporation 17, 133
Mastercard International 41
McDonalds Restaurants 8, 206

Meals for 24 Hours 102
media 31
medicines
    Chinese 146, 149
    Western 149-50
microwave ovens 93
military power 4
millionaire class 24
Ministry of Foreign Trade 2
motorcycles 62, 157
    manufacturer 84
MTV 36

Nabisco Foods China Ltd. 54
Nanjing Road East 86
national road system 43
natural resources 100
people 211
new coastal cities 87-94
newspapers and magazines 31, 37, 117, 124, 127
Nokia 139
nursing home 71
nutrition 144

oil 95-7
OTC (over-the-counter) drugs 144, 227

pagers 113, 137-8, 186
Paris of the East 84
Pearl River Delta Region 88
Pepsi 20
personal computers 57, 103-4, 137-40, 156

pharmaceutical industry 12, 45, 149, 194, 298
population 3, 32, 44, 69, 84, 88, 91, 204
private enterprises 23
product niche approach 194-5
public transport 93
Pudong New Area 82-3

Qijing 129, 227
Qu Tong Xing 12

radio 37
railways 42, 223
    mass transit 86
    national system 95
refrigerators and freezers, ownership 215
regulatory environment change 7
Renao 14
rental accommodation 163-4
residential construction 81-2
housing 44, 167
resource-rich regions 94-8, 211
restaurants 102, 133
retail industry 105, 107
rural 69, 75
    consumers 59
    residents 91-2, 179

satellite cities 78-9, 80-87
savings 9, 10
    long term 45
security 115
senior citizens 13, 103

Senior's Day 69
service industry 142-3
sewing machines 62
s-generation 6, 17, 35, 50-9, 76, 126, 170, 176, 180, 227
Shanghai stock exchange 173, 175
Shenyang-Dalian superhighway 111
shopping 53, 105-6, 133, 158
Si He Yuan housing 114, 117, 124
Singapore 79, 84
single-child family 5-7, 21, 32-3
social influences/status 7, 15, 20
Star TV 36
State 161-2
    employees 44, 164
    enterprises 23, 44, 109-11, 163-4, 182, 192, 217
    offices 41
    subsidization 5
State Statistics Bureau 18
status 17, 52, 152-8
stock markets 172-4
Suzhou Chunhua Vacuum Cleaner Factory 84
Suzhou Television Factory 84

Tarin Basin 97
tax 25-6, 169
taxis 135-6
telecommunications 23, 85, 93, 137, 161, 223
telephones 185-6, 208
    cellular 17, 37, 39, 113, 141, 186
    digital 85
    lines 140-2
    mobile 139

switching stations 139
    system 37
television 36, 53-4, 126, 209
    cable 37
theme parks 107
three-dimensional living 100, 228
tourists 31, 67, 108, 112-13, 129
tuition 184

United States 2, 4, 14, 21, 33, 42, 81
urban areas (see also cities) 82
    populations 142
    residents 142

value-niche approach 197-8
vegetables 65, 135, 142, 145, 208
Visa International 41

Walkmans 113
Wal-Mart 195, 208
Walt Disney Company 196
washing machines 209
wealth 15, 154
World Bank 21, 219
World Trade Organization 179

Xiahai 155, 192, 228

Yangzi River Delta 88
Yuan Qin Bu Ru Jin Lin 115
Yung, Larry 7, 120

Zhongcong Food and Convenience Store 102

Continued from page xx

"This is a well documented study of the emergence of China as a consumer society, written from a business perspective by a former resident of China. The book identifies new niche markets and discusses strategies for doing business in China. Of particular interest is Mr Li's description of China's emerging "s-generation", those consumer-oriented products of China's one-child policy, who, in his view, will make China one of the major consumer markets of the 21st century. Mr Li uses extensive personal anecdotes and draws upon a large network of Chinese friends, relatives and business associates to produce a readable and authoritative study that should be read widely."

Bernard Michael Frolic
Director, Joint Centre for Asia Pacific Studies
University of Toronto-York University

"To know that China is changing is not enough. To understand these changes is imperative. Conghua Li's incisive and stimulating book explores the reasons behind the consumer revolution and its fascinating future direction. In a style as rich and colourful as China itself, he provides a vital source of information for anyone contemplating doing business in China and, indeed, for those of us who are already in there."

Matthew W Barrett
Chairman & CEO, Bank of Montreal

"**China: The Consumer Revolution** ranks as one of the most detailed analyses to date of the shifts in Chinese society introduced by the market."

Far Eastern Economic Review